"You *Have* to Go to School ... You're the *Teacher!*"

I dedicate this book to

Michael—the love of my life
Felicia—my daughter and best friend
Peggy and Irving Rosenblum—in memory

"You *Have* to Go to School . . . You're the *Teacher!*"

200 Tips to Make Your Job Easier and More Fun

Renee Rosenblum-Lowden

CORWIN PRESS, INC.
A Sage Publications Company
Thousand Oaks, California

For information address:

Corwin Press, Inc.
A Sage Publications Company
2455 Teller Road
Thousand Oaks, California 91320
E-mail: order.corwin@sagepub.com

SAGE Publications Ltd.
6 Bonhill Street
London EC2A 4PU
United Kingdom

SAGE Publications India Pvt. Ltd.
M-32 Market
Greater Kailash I
New Delhi 110 048 India

Printed in the United States of America

Library of Congress Cataloging-in-Publication Data

Rosenblum-Lowden, Renee.
    You have to go to school—you're the teacher: 200 tips to make
your job easier and more fun / author, Renee Rosenblum-Lowden.
        p.   cm.
    Includes bibliographical references.
    ISBN 0-8039-6555-9 (cloth : acid-free paper). — ISBN
    0-8039-6556-7 (pbk. : acid-free paper)
    1. Teachers—United States. 2. Teaching—United States.
3. First-year teachers—United States. I. Title.
LB1775.2.R67 1997
371.1′02—dc21   96-51288

97 98 99 00 01 02 03 10 9 8 7 6 5 4 3 2

This book is printed on acid-free paper.

Production Editor:	S. Marlene Head
Production Assistant:	Janet L. Westenberg
Typesetter & Designer:	Andrea D. Swanson
Cover Designer:	Marcia R. Finlayson

Contents

Foreword

Most teacher training programs revolve around preparing the pre-service teacher to present a mass of information for the learners' mastery. The course work is rigorous, and teachers usually approach their classes academically confident in their knowledge of subject area, curriculum and instruction, philosophy of education, language development, social and technological change, and adolescent development. In practice, however, this method of teaching is tremendously limiting both to teachers and students because it tends to produce teachers who lecture and students who are expected to listen, take notes, and memorize information. Students' feelings, attitudes, and beliefs toward learning are largely ignored; such students become passive and discontent participants in their own education.

As educators, we are realizing more and more the importance of a balanced approach to teaching: one in which students and teachers are active participants within the classroom and where the emphasis is placed on the development of the whole child—where collaboration, not competition; mutual respect, not power; self-management, not punishment; and participation, not isolation provide the stimulus for our students to develop personally and academically so that they are eager to take responsibility for their own growth and learning and to realize their full potential.

In *"You Have to Go to School . . . You're the Teacher!,"* Renee Rosenblum-Lowden shares her thoughts, ideas, and experiences about students and teachers; about learning and teaching; and about how, within a positive, success-oriented classroom environment, these roles and processes are not rigidly defined but, instead, are shared.

Ms. Rosenblum-Lowden's balanced approach to teaching is extremely timely. In the introduction, she notes that the intent of the book is to provide preservice, new, and experienced teachers with commonsense strategies that will help them to create and develop an environment that is conducive to effective teaching and successful learning. She has certainly accomplished her goals. Ms. Rosenblum-Lowden's tips will help teachers to create, together with their students, a positive classroom based on respect and trust.

The insightful suggestions and strategies are categorized into eight sections, beginning with teacher behaviors that denote teacher as leader, which then facilitates teacher and students working together. She continues with the importance of students being empowered through responsibility, and—perhaps the most essential concept of all—honest and sensitive communication within the classroom as a vehicle for both teacher and student to understand and appreciate one another personally and academically. Ms. Rosenblum-Lowden ends with a section on the significance of parental support to a student's academic success and offers advice on how to enlist that parental support to meet common goals.

Ms. Rosenblum-Lowden presents her tips as though she is speaking directly to the reader. Her sense of humor is inherent and is evident throughout this collection. Her friendly, relaxed, and flexible voice invites you to share her excitement and passion for teaching by experimenting with her ideas. Ms. Rosenblum-Lowden has taught various grade levels in diversified schools for over 25 years. Her global and specific educational convictions are rooted in her respect for and commitment to students. Her strong beliefs in the ability and success of all students, plus the importance of students being taught by positive, effective, and nurturing teachers, provide the basis for all her work.

BARBARA PEREA
Instructor and Student Teacher Supervisor
San Francisco State University

Acknowledgments

I would like to thank the following people:

- Pearl Newman, my first principal, who taught me one of the best lessons of my career. After my first year of teaching, she offered me a special program, telling me I was one of the best teachers she had ever seen. I looked at her modestly and said, "I'm not really that good." She asked me if I would go to a doctor who said he wasn't really that good. She added, "You're good. Don't deny it." So to show I learned that lesson I will tell you right now, "This book is really good!"

- The staff of Enrich—The School for Social Action, for proving that a good team can do anything. We came as close to a perfect educational experience as I have ever experienced. Thanks to Michelle Fratti for giving us the freedom to create an incredible school.

- Bill Ma, for allowing me to continue my course on prejudice awareness and for being so supportive.

- Sara Mercer, Muriel Rozin, and the student teachers at San Francisco State and Columbia University Teachers College, for making me believe that my strategies were important to share and for encouraging me to write this book.

- My husband Michael for listening to all my school stories, offering great suggestions, and rescuing me every time I thought my book went into cyberspace.

- My daughter Felicia, for sharing her enormous gift for teaching with her students, as well as supplying me with so many creative strategies of her own.

- My father, who told me a cute joke many years ago—which is now the title of this book—and my mother, who told anyone who would listen what a good teacher I was. I only wish they were here today.
- All my students who have brought me so much happiness and enriched my life so much over the past 25 years. I hope they are living healthy and productive lives.

About the Author

Renee Rosenblum-Lowden has taught children and adolescents for more than 25 years in the New York City school system. She has developed a curriculum called Understanding Prejudice, using consciousness-raising techniques and incorporating her training in conflict resolution. She was selected by the NYC Board of Education to train teachers in this subject.

Ms. Rosenblum-Lowden conducts workshops for improving communication with children and adolescents, using nonconfrontational strategies for parents and teachers. Having taught family living and sex education classes, she has unique insights into the needs of her students.

Currently, she is sharing her love for teaching with new teachers and student teachers at various universities, strengthening their skills in making classrooms safe and fun—while always being in control— and then showing them how to create a prejudice-free classroom.

Ms. Rosenblum-Lowden did her undergraduate work at Long Island University and studied at The New School for Social Research and New York University. She continues to be a social activist.

She lives in Brooklyn, New York, and Riegelsville, Pennsylvania, with her husband Michael and their dog, Susan B. Anthony. Her daughter Felicia has taken the baton and is teaching high school in Maryland.

Introduction

A funny thing happened on my way to giving a seminar on a curriculum I developed called Prejudice Awareness. . . .

My daughter Felicia, a student teacher at San Francisco State University, talked about my course with her fellow students. Her classmates kept saying that they would love to hear more about it, which led her professor to invite me to address the graduate student teachers. I gladly leapt at the opportunity, as it was a wonderful excuse to see my daughter. (I don't need an "excuse" to see her, but I do have to justify the 3,000-mile plane trip!)

Well, I planned everything I was going to say but lived in perpetual fear that I would stand up there and re-create some of those awkward moments from what seemed a lifetime ago—when my daughter was a cringing preteen and teenager being humiliated by everything I said and everything I did. I had to keep reminding myself that it was *her* idea to invite me.

When the big night came and I was about to speak, I realized I had left my note cards in the computer room, which was now locked. While Felicia was getting the security guards to open the door to retrieve my notes (and hence, rescue *me*), I was sure that her memories of being embarrassed by me were alive and well in her mind. While she was gone, I noticed all the anxieties that those in her class were sharing among themselves about their own students, the other teachers, their lack of control, and their insecurities in general. I remembered those days and those anxieties.

When I finally began speaking, I looked at them and said, "When I was a new teacher, I asked myself what *I* would want in a teacher if I were one of the students. I knew I would want someone to teach me in an environment that was fun, yet demanding. I hope I did that.

"Then when I became a mother, I asked myself what *I* would want in a mother. I knew I would want someone to be nurturing and to encourage me to believe in myself. I hope I did that.

"Now, tonight, I look at you—new student teachers—and I ask myself yet again, What would *I* want if I were sitting where you are? I would want a real live classroom teacher—a person who has 175 children passing through her classroom every day and has all kinds of strategies to cope with the daily routines and crises that occur—to tell me her 'tricks of the trade.' "

Their heads were nodding so furiously, I knew I was right on target. For the next 2 hours, I shared with them the skills I had accumulated from my contact with so many thousands of young people between 8 and 17 years of age, and from the wisdom I had amassed by having students share their journals and personal thoughts with me. I have also led parent–teacher workshops for many years and was trained in the specialty area of conflict resolution, and I was able to draw on those experiences. After sharing teaching strategies for 2 hours, I discussed my course on prejudice for another 2 hours. And guess what? My daughter winked and gave me two thumbs up. Puberty was over . . . I hadn't humiliated her!

Since that day I have shared my strategies and ideas in workshops with countless other teachers who provided valuable feedback and encouragement. This book has evolved out of that process.

My goal in writing this book is to give teachers the book I wish I'd had when I was first struggling in the classroom—a "teacher-friendly" book to tell me what to expect, how to make my classroom a place that students can't wait to get to and where they want to learn; a commonsense book with a sense of humor, written by someone who has been in the classroom—and who loved every day of it.

In this book there are over 200 strategies to help preservice, new, and experienced teachers develop rapport with students and manage everyday school problems. Major topics include how to start a successful year; how to help students learn responsibility; how to communicate with honesty and fairness; how to build students' confidence; how to prevent confrontation and showdowns; and how to work effectively with parents and school staff.

To all teachers who are looking for new strategies, I hope I provide that for you. I am sure there are some strategies to which you will take exception, but I hope there are many more that you will try and find effective. To all new teachers, I congratulate you on choosing a wonderfully fulfilling career, and I hope my experiences and strategies will help you. Remember, a few of these might work for you, and you will probably invent some for yourself that may be even more successful. Good luck—and make a difference!

RENEE ROSENBLUM-LOWDEN

Mother: Get up, it's time to go to school.

Son: I don't want to go.

Mother: But you have to go to school!

Son: I'm afraid the kids won't like me, and I don't want to go!

Mother: You have to go to school!

Son: I'm too nervous.

Mother: You *have* to go to school . . . You're the *teacher!*

TIPS FOR NEW AND STUDENT TEACHERS

It has often been said that the most creative ideas come from the beginners, not the experts.

People who have been teaching a long time are often called "experts"; some are, and some are not. There are some teachers who have to duck paper airplanes (on a good day) who are considered experts merely because they have been teaching forever. Not so! Most of you are recently out of school and heavily armed with this wonderful strength I call "unjaded idealism." New teachers, fresh out of teaching programs, have shared all kinds of wonderful strategies and philosophies.

Don't be afraid to experiment, and don't be afraid to use all that creativity you know you have. It takes a real short time for a truly talented teacher to become an "expert."

1

Odds and Ends for Beginners

Put Loved Ones on Notice

The first few weeks of teaching are probably going to be filled with stress. Plead with your friends and family to bear with you. You may be short with them, and you may perhaps even use them to vent what you didn't vent in the classroom. Warn them that you will probably fall asleep the second you get home and perhaps sleep through a good part of the weekend.

There will be days when you will have loads of "adorable" stories about "adorable" students. I will warn you of something your loved ones may be too kind to tell you. You may be *boring* them. It's like someone telling you about a neighbor running off with someone else. Unless you know the neighbor, who cares? If you notice their eyes rolling, it may be time to change the subject. But don't worry, there really are many people who will love to hear your stories. (Other teachers who know your students serve as fine audiences.)

Your Students Didn't Sleep Last Night Either!

You may have not slept a wink before your first day, but neither did many of your colleagues and most of your students. No matter how many years we have been teaching, the first day of school always arouses some anxiety. There is a good chance you will toss and turn and then be panicked that you will fall asleep right at your desk. Relax! When the adrenaline kicks in, you will be just fine. The reality is that your students are so into themselves, they don't notice your anxieties.

Dress Like a Grown-Up

Oh, I can't believe I'm saying this! When I began teaching, I prided myself on being a nonconformist and insisted on wearing jeans to school. But this was a problem, because I was young when I began teaching and I looked close in age to my students. And guess what? They treated me as if I were one of them.

It may sound nice, but as the authority in the classroom, you have to distance yourself a bit. One way to do so is to dress the part. Dressing like a professional gives you a head start in your classroom. It says, "I am the teacher and you are the student." Studies have shown that discipline techniques work better when a teacher looks more professional. I didn't believe them until the day I had to get dressed up to go somewhere after school and found an indefinable difference in how my students reacted to me. It was definitely positive.

A friend of mine who teaches junior high school students was told by one of his students, "You must really like us. You come to school all dressed up, as though you are going someplace special."

Eventually you can dress however you feel is appropriate, but in the beginning I suggest you dress like the professional you are. Also, keep in mind that many adolescent students develop "crushes" on their teachers, so I'm even going to go so far as to tell you to dress conservatively.

Students Do Get Crushes

It happens! No matter how young the student, you can become the object of his or her adoration. Please be sensitive to this, as these fragile little hearts are easily broken by a patronizing laugh. Be careful to keep a distance, because students often become very possessive and even get upset at the thought of you having a social life.

I had a student (who came up to my waist) who told me his dream of beating up my husband. When I asked him why, he said he just didn't like him. (By the way, he'd never met him!)

With older students, especially high schoolers, teachers have to be especially conscious about not sending out signals, or responding to those being sent.

Overplan

As a new teacher, it is impossible to gauge how long your first day's lesson plans will last. You should have your introductions, course expectations, classroom and school rules, temporary seating arrangements, and some homework assignments prepared. It's a good idea to have additional lessons "just in case." I have had years when I never even got up to the rules and other years when I seemed to be done in a minute and a half. The dynamics of a group vary so much that it is impossible to plan a 45-minute lesson and expect each group to react the same way. Remember, it is hard to "wing it," especially with a brand-new group. There are always perceptive students who know you are not prepared and can make you look as if you are not in control.

Have 2 hours of lessons for your 1-hour class. It's a great habit to get into. Remember, if you aren't prepared, how can you expect your students to be? My money is on you, though, because a new teacher usually overplans in the beginning.

Everyone Else's Plans Are Better

While we are talking about plans, I hear so many new teachers tell me they are sure everyone else has better lesson plans. They always feel theirs are not good enough. Don't fret. Those you admire are probably wondering what great ideas you've got up your sleeve. Your plans are probably fine, but self-doubt can be a great motivator. Whenever I hear people complain about inexperienced teachers, I chuckle to myself. You see, I love working with new teachers because I usually think their plans are better than mine!

Ask Teachers for Help

Never hesitate to ask another teacher for help. I have discovered that some teachers claim they never need help, even though their classrooms may be in total chaos. Sometimes the ego gets in the way of asking for help, especially as one gets older. So quick, while you are new and humble and your ego allows you to admit when you need a hand, reach for it! Teachers love to help newer teachers, and you may learn someone else's "tricks of the trade" and use them in your classroom. Very often a teacher will be able to tell you just how to handle the girl who hums off-key just to annoy you, or that boy who specializes in "snowing" teachers. I am sure that when you are experienced, you will extend the same courtesy to some new protégé who is insecurely entering into our profession.

The Mentor Teacher

Student teachers always ask me how I suggest they tell their mentoring teacher that what he or she is doing is wrong. *Well, don't even think about it!* You are a guest in your mentor's classroom and should behave that way. We have to look at our mentor teachers as we would our parents. You know, we are stuck with them unless they are absolutely awful and only then can we usually do something about it. However, a good idea might be to offer "suggestions" or ask if you may try something a little differently. A good mentor teacher usually asks for your input, at which time you may feel free to express yourself. You are there to learn from, not to teach, your mentor, even though we both know you have so much to share.

One of my student teachers had a wonderful outlook. She had taught under a rigid autocrat who terrorized his students and even scared her. She said, "I learned from him what *not* to do!"

hypocritical to punish your students for tardiness, while you stroll in at your leisure. None of this "Do as I say, not as I do" stuff works here.

Enthusiasm Is Caught, Not Taught

We want this year to be exciting and productive for our students as well as for ourselves. So first we have to psych ourselves to bubble with motivating enthusiasm. How do you accomplish that? Simple: You are well prepared, have the most exciting lessons ready to spark those eager minds, and realize that if you don't want to be there, neither will they. Tell them how you are looking forward to a great year together. You might even ask them what they expect from their teachers. (Of course, you will be everything they say and more!)

Friendly, But Not Buddies

In the beginning of the school year, a teacher is always being tested. That is when I tell my students, "My job is to teach, not to be a buddy." You don't want to be a pushover because kids can be merciless. I have seen teachers try to be "buddies" with their students on Day 1. Believe it or not, that is not what your students want. They have their peers and no matter how "cool" you are, you are not their pal.

I always tell kids who become too chummy that we can be friendly, but not friends. Too many teachers don't do this because they are afraid their students won't like them. Trust me, they will.

If you don't define the line, they get confused when they are disrespectful and you in turn call a parent to complain about their disrespect. After I tell them in my sternest voice that my job is to teach them, I smile and assure them they will love me within a few weeks. (When I feel they're getting too chummy, I threaten them by telling them I will hang out with them and complain about my arthritis. That always does it!)

First Name Versus Surname

Whether to use first names or surnames is a matter of personal preference. I went through the "Renee" stage and thought it was just fine, until I noticed we were becoming equals in the classroom. The reality is that we cannot all be in charge. It is only you, the teacher, who can assume this role, and distancing yourself by using your title is a quite benign way of doing that. With very young children, your mere stature does that. You can always later allow them to call you by your first name after they've called you by your surname. Rarely can you do the reverse.

Again, it's totally up to you—unless, of course, your school has a policy about first names.

Personal Records Debate

This may be unusual, and some teachers may disagree with me, but (except in the case of special-needs students) I do not read my students' academic/social record for a few weeks. I have found that reading comments from other teachers will slant the way I view a given student. You can tell me from today to tomorrow that the record won't affect how you perceive an individual, but, take my word, you will be prejudiced. If you hear, for instance, that a student is hostile, you will be anticipating it.

I know kids who did really fine work, although their records indicated that they were 2 years behind in reading. I had to fight myself not to lower my expectations. I am not suggesting you *not* read the records, because it is clearly important for you to learn as much as you can about all of your students. I only encourage you to form your own opinions first.

This does not hold true for the medical part of the record. That should be looked at immediately. It is important for you to know right away if a student needs medication or has certain limitations. There was a boy in my third-grade class who had a minor heart condition, and his physical activities had to be curtailed. Had I not read his record, I could have endangered his health because he would certainly be the last one to tell me he couldn't run 246 laps around the gymnasium. Most kids don't want to appear different from their peers.

You will, of course, keep this information confidential and never embarrass a child by referring to it unnecessarily, even in private.

Going on Automatic

Before I discuss strategies on how to avoid confrontation, let me try to assuage the guilt I am sure you will have for the times you "lose it." We all go on automatic occasionally. What I mean is that we yell, say things we should not say, and, in general, become the teacher we vowed we never would become. Come on, it will happen and it is OK *once in a while.* You are human and therefore have permission to err. The only request I have is for you to tell yourself you went on automatic and try to learn something from it. When I would go on automatic, I would say to myself, "Oh, well, I goofed." Realizing that is half the battle. Think of all those teachers who do the same thing and do not see the negative impact it has on their students.

And while we are talking about going on automatic, our students have to know that we too have our limits and have a right to our anger. A good suggestion is to confide in your class that you are feeling angry, tell them why, and tell them what *they* can do about the situation. If they want a fair classroom, they too have to contribute toward making it feel safe and not assume it is solely your job.

Don't Take Their Behavior Personally

As wonderful as you are, their peers' opinions are the ones that really count. I have had students ask if they could stay around and chat with me after school, only to ignore me the next day when they were among their friends. How could they like me so much at 3:00 on Monday and ignore me at 9:00 on Tuesday? Easy, their friends are more important. Don't panic. They'll be back and hopefully you will greet them with open arms because you are the one who makes them feel safe and helps them learn.

You Can't Win 'Em All

If you are the sensitive type, you feel disappointed when your students don't like you or the lesson on which you worked so hard. It is important not to take things personally because most times they are not personal, although on occasion they are. Some may think your approach to teaching is the pits, and may think your style was created to put them to sleep. (See Am I Boring? on page 39.) Well, that does happen, and unless most of your students feel that way, I wouldn't worry. If most of your students manage to stay awake, learn, and even miraculously laugh at your jokes, just enjoy the feat of pleasing most. You can't please everyone.

3

They're Here

The Rush to Seats

I have a wonderful win–win solution to this. I let them sit where they choose, but as soon as they are seated I explain that the seating arrangement is not permanent and will be changed. There might be a moan or two, but they usually accept that their seats are temporary. Live with the seating for a couple of days and if it seems to be working, tell them you trust their judgment and you will let them sit where they chose. Suddenly you are considered the greatest teacher who ever lived because they feel you gave them something. If the seating arrangement has disruptive kids stimulated by other disruptive kids (or a student being intimidated by a nearby classmate), then you go back to your original deal. You are fair because you explained the plan up front, and their moaning will probably be kept to a minimum.

A Seating Idea

You can experiment with seating in many ways. Some people like to cluster their students, while others prefer traditional rows. I personally prefer the horseshoe, or the upside-down U. Basically, the class is in a semicircle and I am in the front of the room. There is a trick to this structure that helps with discipline problems. When I first began, I thought I was real clever by putting the disruptive kids on both sides of the room, rather than next to one another. *Don't do it!* They'll be facing one another—free to make faces, call out to each other, and act out every other possible human distraction. I finally learned to handle it by seating them all on one side, separated by more attentive students. The troublemakers then cannot see one another and are more likely to focus on you. Another advantage is that you can be a physical presence either by standing close to inattentive students or standing at opposite ends of the room and maintaining eye contact with anyone being disruptive.

If you have a class full of difficult students, I wouldn't try this seating plan, but if there is a good balance of students, this arrangement can get everyone involved in a positive way.

Don't Seat by Height—or Gender

It is humiliating for the student who doesn't fit into his or her height norm to be singled out for this characteristic. Don't worry about the smaller kids—they can see from anywhere and if they can't they will let you know. The last thing a student wants is for you to focus on his or her lack of inches (or abundance thereof—tall kids can feel gawky, too!).

Lining up your students in size order is also not necessary. Try letting them line up by themselves or in alphabetical order (or reverse alphabetical order for those Zimmers who are always last).

Speaking of seating, why is it that we would never segregate children by race, yet we insist on segregating by gender? Even if it is what the students prefer, we as educators have got to stop perpetuating the myth that males and females are "opposites." We have to foster interaction as early as possible and not let each sex see the other one as "the enemy" or "the other." Perhaps if this is done in the earlier grades, boys and girls will become more enriched by each other by the time they enter the middle grades.

Interchange Gender Pronouns

I grew up thinking everyone was male unless otherwise stated. My teachers referred to everyone as *he* (except ballet dancers, nurses, secretaries, and "lady" doctors). The English language should be inclusive, because young girls and boys do not understand generic language. They take everything literally and internalize what they hear. So the boy who never hears a nurse referred to as *he* or the girl who never hears a scientist referred to as *she* is hearing gender roles being assigned by us when we should not be doing that.

One year, a seventh grader confessed that as a little boy, he always thought girls were lucky because they didn't have to worry about getting eaten by "man"-eating sharks. It was a wonderful example of how young children are so literal.

You will notice throughout this guide that I alternate masculine and feminine pronouns. You may also be aware that when "she" is used, it is more conspicuous. Hopefully, one day we will no longer notice.

Put Your Name—and Phone Number?—on the Board

Needless to say, your name goes on the board *first thing*. Since you are the boss, it's real important that they know who you are. But you're probably asking, "Why in heaven's name would I give these total strangers my home phone number?" You probably have visions of half the school calling and asking if your refrigerator is running and then telling you to go catch it! There may be those who would actually do that, but the amazing discovery I've made is that when they have permission to call, they usually don't unless it is school related.

I do this for two reasons. First, they feel it is such an act of trust that you would actually let them call you at home. I make it very clear that they may call only if it is very important and they must speak to me. They may not call about homework assignments because they have a homework buddy for that. (See Homework Buddies on page 29.) I also explain that I go to bed early and not to call after 9 o'clock. Second, I am so generous with my number because if they wanted to make a prank call, all they'd have to do is look my number up in the phone book!

In the beginning there are usually a few kids who will call on a pretense just to hear my "at-home" voice. Occasionally, I've gotten calls from kids in crisis. Very seldom did I get "mystery calls," and the few that I did get may have been students or just people dialing a wrong number and not using proper phone etiquette.

This is just my experience. Many teachers are not comfortable with this and therefore should not do it. (It's easy not to if your name is Smith!)

Tangible Class Guidelines and Rules

It is important that you think through what you expect from your class and what they should expect from you. You can explain everything to them in detail, but it helps to have the rules in writing, in their hands (and, on the bulletin board). You can give them two sets. One they must keep in their notebooks, and the other they and their parents must sign and return to you to keep on file. During the year, when a student says, "I didn't know you would fail me because I didn't do 188 homeworks," you can pull out her signed agreement. It is important that the parents sign this agreement because some parents have been known to try to put teachers on the defensive, saying they were not informed of certain requirements their child had to fulfill. You can show them the signed contract and this usually ends the confrontation.

You Own the Limelight

The beginning of the school year is the time to establish yourself as the person in charge.

Observe how peer groups form and how you sometimes unwittingly become part of this process. I have seen some kids be perceived as "cool" if they can put down the teacher. If they are successful, you're in big trouble. Common behavior patterns of this kind of student are to yell out to the teacher, mutter under his breath, or just engage other kids in a conversation while you are right there at the front of the room being just as nice as you can be. What to do? Sometimes a quick glance at the disruptive student may suffice. If not, you may have to do the unthinkable, and that might involve embarrassing the student. Stop and explain to the "cool" kid that under no circumstances do you talk over anyone else and that you will protect that right for everyone in the room. (To some, this can be terribly intimidating.)

If you talk over a conversation, the noise level just rises and, before you know it, no one can be heard and you are yelling. I am not saying that a classroom should always be quiet—I would hardly want that—but when the lesson is teacher directed, the teacher has the floor.

Good educational experiences usually encourage enthusiastic talking and *that* is music to the ears.

Alternative to Screaming #1: The Stare

Screaming should be avoided at all costs, because if you yell all the time, trust me, you will soon not be heard. There are a few simple strategies that might deter you from committing verbal violence (and prevent you from getting a serious case of laryngitis). One is the infamous stare. Locking eyes with a student who is distracting you or the class often gets him to refrain immediately. Once it is obvious that the student has picked up your signal, you can even offer a wink. It shows that you are not angry anymore and that you appreciate the display of respect.

Alternative to Screaming #2: The "Excuse Me" Smile

Another technique is the one we all heard from our teachers. You know, where you just stop what you are doing and say in the sternest voice you can muster, "*Excuse me*, but *I* am talking." There will always be that student who responds, "You're excused," in which case I suggest you try a smile and go on.

The smile, by the way, should be a common expression on your face. A warm smile means a warm teacher—or so they think. I am not giving you permission to grin all day, because you may then come off as *weird*, but a sour face is never fun to be around, and certainly not to be endured for a full school year.

Alternative to Screaming #3: The Lowered Voice

I have mentioned that you should not get into the habit of speaking over your students. The trick is to use a lowered voice.

When you are teaching, you may hear just a slight buzz in the classroom, and your tendency will be to *raise* your voice just a bit. But soon you'll hear just a little more talking, and you'll raise your voice just a little more. When you finally hear the roar of the class and the shriek coming out of your throat, you'll know you put this strategy into practice too late.

So speak a little softer as soon as you hear that initial buzz. When people are straining to hear, they stop talking and often tell the others around them to be quiet.

Alternative to Screaming #4: The Art of Gestures

Another alternative to raising your voice is to gesture. There are many gestures that you should show your students within the first couple of weeks of the school year that will save your body and soul wear and tear. Here are some examples: finger on your lips for silence, snapping fingers to attract attention or to hurry up a dawdler (beware that in some cultures this is considered rude—see Cultural Differences on page 92), thumbs-up for approval, and "tsk, tsk" for disapproval. My favorite is raising my hand and having the class automatically copy my movement by raising their hands. At the same time, they automatically get quiet and, for the life of me, I don't know why this works. I am beginning to believe there is a muscle that connects a slowly rising hand to a quieted mouth, although I have yet to prove this anatomically.

You Can Always Ease Up

It is tempting to be permissive from the beginning, because no one wants to start out the year with all those "mean" rules. But unless you establish them early on, you will pay the consequences. If you say there will be homework every day, they will groan but expect it. On the day you give them no homework, you'll be seen as a saint.

But the reverse can be catastrophic. Try telling kids you won't give them homework on the weekends and then do just the opposite. You will have a potential student revolution on your hands.

Sit With Your Students

Too often we stand in front of the room and just lecture. It can be boring and sometimes even a little intimidating, but, alas, that's where the blackboard or the overhead is, and standing there brings the focus to you. But on occasion, I pull up a chair and sit with my students, usually while reading a story or having a class discussion. Sitting at their level makes everyone feel more comfortable. I have found that this strategy encourages more students to participate.

Also, sitting on top of a desk, rather than standing, accomplishes the same thing and puts off your need to purchase those less attractive "sensible shoes."

Fun Introductions

Depending on the age of the student, there are many ways they can introduce themselves. I'll just throw a few at you.

Younger children can say their names and add a noun, as in "Linda the Lion." Another way is to have kids reveal one thing that is special about themselves (or makes them different from others in your class).

Students can pair up and find out as much as they can about one another and then introduce their partners. Some students simply find it is easier to talk about others rather than about themselves. This exercise might be easier if you have a prepared list of suggested questions.

Another pairing strategy is to have each twosome list a few things they have in common and a few ways in which they are totally different from one another. If there is an odd number of students, go ahead and jump in and be the other half of a pair.

A real fun exercise is to have each child write one truth about himself and one lie and have the class guess which is which. It's a good icebreaker because the kids love it and it is easy for you to take part.

If you feel more comfortable with traditional methods, you can give them a written assignment wherein they introduce themselves on paper and read what they wrote aloud. This is also a subtle way to assess their writing skills.

Now and Later Cards

Now and Later Cards first introduce the students to you at the beginning of the year and later show how they have changed by the end of the year.

You begin by giving out small index cards and composing questions that will give you insight into who your students are. Examples might include

What is your favorite subject?

What is your pet peeve?

What do you hope will happen to you this year?

What music do you like?

Save the cards and on the last day of school, return the cards to them. They always laugh because half of the answers hardly describe them at the end of the year. I have seen teens cringe because they liked the "wrong" rock group in September and can't believe how uncool they were.

To Touch or Not to Touch

I have to be real careful about what I write here because of how sensitive this issue has become. Sometimes I hear comments such as, "A kindergarten teacher can't even wipe a child's runny nose because she will be sued." I hardly believe that, and I think anyone who is in the classroom knows her safety boundaries early on.

I am more concerned with older students who are going through puberty and are uncomfortable with their sexuality. And I have to add that, unfortunately, male teachers have to be more conscious— and cautious—about this than females. Women by nature (and with societal permission) tend to touch people of both genders in benign ways. But because of the few male teachers who have overstepped their boundaries, men are very often viewed with suspicion by both boys and girls.

Male teachers are in a power position and may feel completely comfortable touching girls, but in more cases than not, the student will feel extremely uncomfortable. (Male teachers rarely touch young males, but for some reason they think it is OK to touch a female. Don't take the chance.)

We had a teacher who used to ask the fifth-grade girls for a hug. He was a very nice teacher, but I had to tell him that his behavior was inappropriate. He was outraged at me and accused me of being out of line, but those girls who had complained to me thanked me for my action. (See Confronting Other Teachers on page 105).

Lifesaving Referral Slips

When there is an accident or a major infraction, teachers must put it in writing and on record. Make sure your statements are nonjudgmental and contain only the facts without personal interpretation.

Sometimes, because we are so overwhelmed with all our responsibilities as a teacher, we put off writing the report and forget about it. Try not to. Very often parents will side with their child no matter what and will accuse you of picking on the student. It is helpful if a teacher is able to retrieve a file and show parents that the child has past offenses that are documented. According to law, you must document accidents because lawsuits are becoming increasingly common. Basically, I am just telling you to protect yourself.

I had this horrendously disruptive and hurtful child in my class. When I spoke to the mother, she initially expressed concern. As time went by her concern shifted to "getting the teachers" rather than getting help for her son. He had set a fire in the bathroom, and all she wanted to see was the documentation. Rather than address the serious issues regarding her son's behavior, she would put me on the defensive. I was stunned to see how few teachers had written up reports on him (though we would share "Jimmy" stories over lunch, trying to find solutions to help him). This mother attacked me verbally, saying I just didn't like her child. (More about those parents later.) Had I had all the documentation, I might have been able to get this child help. He eventually ended up getting stabbed instead of getting the counseling he desperately needed.

Yowks! 5 Minutes Left

It was bound to happen. You had it perfectly planned—a 40-minute lesson for your 30-minute time slot. But guess what? It bombed! You lost their interest, you tried every trick in the book to resuscitate your lesson, and you found that you still had time to spare. Not enough time to start something new, but too much time to sit and wait for the bell to ring.

What to do? I don't care what grade you're teaching: Play Simon Says. It's a sure crowd pleaser. If you want to be more cerebral, play Hangman, and to make sure they enjoy it, divide the room in half and make it a team competition. My Hangman game is always a sentence, rather than a word. (It depends on how many minutes you have left to ad lib!) Reading a story that can be picked up at any point is another good idea. You know you have a winner when the bell rings and they groan.

End the First Day on an Up Note

Make sure the day ends on a positive note. You may have told them about the term projects they will be getting and given them lots of books to take home to cover. But today you can be so kind by announcing that they will only have a short assignment, because you want them to be well rested for a great day tomorrow. Your day ends, hopefully, with smiling students who feel you are the fairest person in the world, and who will be indebted to you forever—OK, maybe not forever, but a few hours are better than nothing!

4

They're Gone and You Survived!

Everything Can Be Redone

Even before your students come in, keep in mind that nothing you do or say is written in stone. You may have great strategies that you just know will work and suddenly you find everything you said and did bombed! Don't fret. Tomorrow is another day and you can redo whatever has to be redone. If your students give you the "But you said yesterday" routine, explain to them you were not happy with the results and that one good thing about being the teacher is that you can change what you think needs to be modified. Period!

You're Not a Shrink

During the day you may have encountered a student who you are sure belongs anywhere but in your class. Remember, unless you are a trained counselor or therapist, you must know your professional and legal limitations. We all have students who create trouble for themselves and others. If their behavior concerns you, I strongly suggest that you refer them to the school guidance counselor, who is trained to deal with these issues. If you have students writing journals or if you are told something in confidence that you think needs professional attention, you may have to betray that student's confidence (see Journals on page 64). Students may talk about suicide, abuse, drugs, depression, or other serious matters that require a professional. You are a teacher, not a psychologist. It is better to betray a confidence than to risk a child harming herself because your judgment was wrong.

Go Home and Chill Out

My daughter joined me at one of my student teacher seminars. She was, after all, a seasoned teacher of 6 months. (She was actually nominated for Teacher of the Year in her high school during that time—OK, I am bragging, but I am a mother!) Her advice to the new teachers was to go home after they finished their first week and just indulge themselves. She suggested they take a bubble bath, read a book with absolutely no redeeming value, or just go to the movies with friends. She encouraged them to divorce themselves from the job for a little while. I had forgotten how consuming it could be, and from the smiles in the audience, I knew she totally understood where they were coming from. I think that is wonderful advice for even the most seasoned veteran.

HELPING STUDENTS
BE RESPONSIBLE

Our students desperately need order in their lives, and it is up to us to help them by setting limits with them. Limits make them feel safe. When we define limits we are telling our students they cannot venture into water that is too deep. Our students often seem to be irresponsible, so we have to gently show them that every action has a consequence. Following are some strategies that help them assume responsibility as you set well-defined limits with clear consequences.

5

Establishing Routines

Creatures of Habit

I want to stress here the need for routines. This goes for you as well as your students. Schoolchildren are creatures of habit and work beautifully when they know what is expected of them. When they enter my classroom, it is a given that they take their seats as attendance is being taken. Other teachers might allow their students to mill around for a few minutes, but in either case the students know what is expected of them. Homework, classroom chores, and certain structured lessons can easily be routinized. You will find that routines provide you with extra time for constructive teaching, and you'll spend less time giving unnecessary explanations.

The Standardized Notebook

I make all my older students buy a large three-ring binder. I have had more confrontations than I would like with eager students who bought small, two-hole books with reams of non-standard-sized paper. These are usually those students who can least afford it, and who make me seem like the Wicked Witch of the West.

The reality is that small paper is bothersome to grade because it usually falls somewhere under the desk, and most teacher handouts are on standard $8\frac{1}{2}$-by-11-inch paper, which students cannot put in their notebooks because they don't fit. They simply fold them up neatly . . . and they are never seen again.

The "Do Now"

Teachers have been doing the "Do Now" for centuries. The idea is to have a short exercise prepared for students to do as soon as they walk into the room. It sets the tone for learning from the minute they enter. It should be something relatively easy and should not take more than a few minutes.

An example of a Do Now is to have a quote on the board, like the contents of a Hallmark greeting card or a thought-provoking quote such as, "The only time you should look down at someone is when you are helping him or her up." All the students have to do is copy it and write about what it means and how it relates to them. (They need not use a new sheet of paper each time but rather just date each entry and continue from the previous Do Now.) When they've completed the exercise, spend a few more minutes sharing some of their writings with the whole class. In those 5 minutes, the class has gotten settled, notebooks have been opened, and pens are poised for working. Pretty shrewd, huh?

The Aim of "Aim"

I also put the aim for every lesson on the board. It focuses on exactly what you intend to teach. We want our students to come in and settle down right away so that we can begin our activity. When my students walk into the room they automatically look at the board for the "Do Now" and then for the "Aim," which they write down in their notebooks. They know the business of the day and it is a settling routine. They also look for the homework assignment in its usual place on the board. I have had students indignantly reprimand me for not having the "Aim" on the board!

The Homework Spot

It is a good idea to have a short daily homework assignment prepared from Day 1. They'll groan, but don't be put off by it. They expect homework! I always put my assignments in the same spot on the board. When my students walk into my room, they automatically look at the upper left-hand corner of the board. It just makes for an easy routine, and homework becomes something they expect—and should get!

The Importance of Homework

Believe it or not, your students understand that homework is a sign that a teacher cares about them. It is easier *not* to give homework, but we must give challenging assignments. Of equal importance is the manner in which the assignments are treated by the teacher. Are the homework assignments checked? Marked? Discussed? Used in a follow-up lesson?

Homework is also a parent–teacher relationship tool. The homework represents you. Make sure it isn't just busywork, or so difficult that you expect parents to play a major role in it. (See Parents and Homework on page 102.)

Numbering Homework

I always prefer to place my homework assignments in the upper left-hand corner of the chalkboard with the date and the assignment number. I ask a student to copy the date, the assignment, and its number, and post it on a sheet of paper on a bulletin board. When a student misses a homework assignment, all she has to do is look at the sheet and there is the date and the number of the missed assignment.

Often you might have to explain the lesson one-on-one so that the student will be able to do the homework. For example, if the assignment is to write a haiku and the student was absent for that lesson, the assignment per se doesn't mean much without an explanation.

Collecting Homework

Collecting homework can be a time-consuming activity, and we want to save every moment for instruction. To save time, I have large manila envelopes tacked up on bulletin boards. I have students drop the homework assignment into the envelope that has their class or the appropriate subject written on the front, and I collect their work at the end of the day. Ideally, you should collect the homework near your desk so you can write down who is unprepared while the class is quietly working on the "Do Now" assignment.

Homework Buddies

In Put Your Name—and Phone Number?—on the Board (page 14), I suggested you give your students your telephone number. If you were brave enough to do so, I suggest you strongly stress that they may not call you for a homework assignment. That is not your job. You do that during the day, and at night you are entitled to your privacy unless they have an urgent need to speak to you.

To eliminate the problem of missed homework, I have them take the phone numbers of the two people seated next to them. (Make sure they are not their best friends, because they already *have* those phone numbers.) If a student is absent, he has at least two phone numbers of classmates who know the assignments and, therefore, has no excuse for missing any homework.

When to Give Out Worksheets

OK, you have spent hours on a worksheet, but you know there are parts that need to be explained before your students can begin their task. You give the sheet to them right away and tell them not to look at it until you have finished your instruction. Well, that's like giving a beautifully wrapped birthday gift to a child and telling her not to look at it for a few days. Don't count on it!

If students need the sheet for clarification, make sure you get them into the habit of having everyone look at the same place on the paper at the same time. Some will say they didn't hear you explain the rules, but you and I know why. They were reading ahead!

"Bathroom Control"

I hate to be responsible for someone else's bodily functions—it just gives me too much power! When students approach me bobbing up and down, I feel terribly guilty saying they may not leave the room. So I let them be responsible for monitoring their own bathroom habits.

I have a sheet on which they sign their names and write the time and date when they leave the room. I assure them that I trust they are not just leaving the room because I am a bore. However, I do check the sheet, and I can tell at a glance which students are abusing the privilege. I will discuss this issue with these students privately, show them how often they are leaving the room, and question whether they are being responsible or taking advantage of my trust. As a result, they tend to leave the room less often because they know I check the sign-out sheets.

Division of Labor

A teacher always has one or two students who are her right hand (oops, I may get into trouble with left-handed people here). I always have some girls—and it is almost exclusively girls—who will yell at me for having a messy desk, and then proceed to organize it. But in all fairness, a classroom has to have an equal division of labor. I suggest you make a chart and have the class list as many chores as possible. Chores can range from running errands to emptying the pencil sharpener. I ask for volunteers and then I randomly pick students to fill the unassigned task. Each month or so the jobs are changed. Everyone must have a responsibility, and it is up to you to see that no one is being exploited or underutilized. Don't always give girls the tidying jobs and boys the lifting jobs. Girls can take out the garbage and boys can straighten the room. It is a good idea to assign these chores so our students will get used to nongendered roles.

Who Dismisses?

In school or grades in which there are departmentalized classes, a bell usually rings to signal that the period is over. I have my students exercise self-control when the bell rings. They have to wait for *me* to tell them they are dismissed. If I am explaining something when the bell rings, the moment will be lost if I am left standing there babbling to any emptying classroom. Experience has taught me to let them know that "*I* dismiss, not the bell."

It takes time for them to stop instinctively jumping up and rushing out of my room, but this is a rule that I expect them to respect.

It is also an excellent lesson in self-control. Of course, you must be sure to leave enough time for students to get to their next class promptly.

Class Wrap-Ups

A nice touch is to give closure to your lessons. You may ask your students what they liked best, what they learned, what they didn't like, or any other comments relevant to the lesson. This is not meant to be an informal quiz but, rather, a closing discussion on what was accomplished during that period.

I would often tell my students how I felt the lesson went, and sometimes I had to break the news that teachers do not corner the market on being boring. If a class was notably unresponsive or inattentive, I would inform them that they did not participate enough and I found *them* bo-o-o-ring. (But keep a smile on your face so they know you are teasing in a good-natured way.)

6

Empowering Students

We Make Our Own Choices

Our students have to learn that they have choices—we all have choices. Some are easy and some are more difficult. I talk a great deal about consequences. A belief that I hold dear is that every act has a consequence, and that our actions determine how we will live our lives.

I remember a terrific student of mine who was caught threatening other students to give him their homework. He claimed he did it because he was broke and had to work after school, so he didn't have time to do his homework. I pointed out that there were many other students working after school who did not choose to cheat. It was his choice, and he chose to intimidate others and then to portray himself as the victim.

I totally empathized with his problems, but I would not enable him by sanctioning his actions. Too often, teachers feel sorry for students and let things like that slide. I feel that that is an injustice and we have to be tough for the sake of those very children about whom we care so much.

Let Students Set Rules and Consequences

You can ask the class what rules they consider fair. (Don't ask what rules they think are unfair—if you do, you'll be sorry!)

For instance, I ask them what would make a classroom feel safe, and then we brainstorm and compile a list of rules. It is hard for them to complain that the rules *they* set are unfair.

Of course, if you see that they are not being serious and are making rules such as "There should be no homework ever," go back to a dictatorship and declare yourself czar.

The Right to Pass

Were you one of those kids who dreaded having to read aloud in class? I was. I would count the number of people before me and try and find the paragraph I would have to read, and then practice it over and over in my head. By the time it was my turn to read, I thought I was going to have an anxiety attack. I feared making a mistake and having others laugh at me.

To ease this anxiety in your students, give them the right to pass. Once the classroom is safe, you will find that these "passers" will eventually partake in class discussions.

If I find that a student is not participating at all, I have to modify the passing rule. I engage her in a discussion in which there can be no wrong answer. It may be something as simple as "What is your favorite holiday?" If she continues to pass, I'll say, "Come on, please share that with us." I then pick up on the theme and ask follow-up questions about what she does on that holiday, and so forth. In short, getting students to talk about something with which they are familiar initiates them into the world of oral communication in a relatively nonthreatening way.

Tacit Approval

Try to follow me on this one, because it is great when it works. As I mentioned earlier, several of my classes, particularly the ones on prejudice awareness and sex education, required a very "safe" classroom because of the course contents. But how can students feel safe enough to share personal experiences and feelings if they fear being made fun of by their peers?

I write the words *Tacit Approval* on the board, and define the term as unspoken approval. Examples of tacit approval can be snickering, pointing, and winking.

For example, we all know that no one in the room is going to tell the class bully not to pick on the class victim. Yet we all wish he would stop. What we *can* do is refuse to laugh, or look away, or anything else that will make the bully feel self-conscious or less comfortable. We know how we feel when we tell that hysterically funny joke and no one even smiles. We want to crawl away and shrivel up. This is the same feeling the bully experiences when he is not encouraged by others.

In the beginning, you—as the teacher—may have to point out someone who is being unkind and getting support from his class-mates, and show how they are giving tacit approval. Someone eventually says "Stop giving tacit approval" to someone putting down another classmate. I have been doing this for years, and I have seen class after class catch on and become empowered.

I once had a new girl come into my class after having been expelled from another school for hitting a teacher. She sauntered into my room, and when I told her she would need a notebook, she said, "I'll get one if I feel like it, lady." She looked around, waiting for everyone to laugh because, after all, she had put down the teacher. She just got stares, and she fled the room. As I ran after her, I heard my kids saying, "It worked! We didn't give her tacit approval!" I had forgotten about the tacit approval strategy but they hadn't, and suddenly they saw how they could make a difference. Indeed, they were empowered.

One Is a Rat—Ten Is Power

I once had a student who was stealing schoolbags from other students and I was sure that everyone but me knew who was doing it. I naïvely asked them to please tell me who it was.

Here I was asking some poor student to stand up and rat on the toughest bully in school. *Sure!* Finally, the bells went off in my head, and I realized I had asked the impossible. So I said to them, "I do not expect one of you to tell me because you don't want to be perceived as a 'rat.' I understand that. But I also know you all want this terrorism to stop. If ten of you tell me, you then have power. The thief cannot threaten everyone. So if you know who is doing it, please put a note in my mailbox with his or her name and I promise no one will know you told me. However, if I don't get at least ten of you to name the person, I cannot do anything about it. Empower yourselves and prevent yourself or someone else from being victimized."

The next day I had over 20 little scraps of paper from my newly empowered students. Being armed with this information allowed me to confront the student who was stealing and frightening all his classmates, and have him suspended. No more schoolbags were stolen, and the lesson about power in numbers was well learned.

Take note: Don't ask the kids to write down the name while the class is in session. They will hesitate when in the presence of anyone they fear.

The "Many Kids Told Me" Fib

This is the educational equivalent of the Witness Protection Program. We all understand that kids are afraid to tell on one another for fear of retaliation, fear of being ridiculed, or some such reason. Sometimes there is a student who is brave enough to tell you who has been beating up all the kindergarten kids and taking their milk money. At the same time, he or she makes you swear on your life that you will not say who told you.

So how do you confront the bully without evidence and without revealing your source? I tell the bully that *several* classmates told me what they saw, and with all those "witnesses," the bully usually breaks down and confesses. Actually, it is not a fib, just an exaggeration!

Don't Call Home

Don't call home? You are probably thinking, "This woman is telling us not to do what we were taught always to do." Let me clarify.

Unless we were born under a lucky star, we are bound to get that "worst-nightmare" student in one of our classes at one time or another. We also know we are going to have to live with this nightmare for a whole school year. The last thing we want to do is alienate that student at the beginning of the term because, whether or not we want to believe it, some students can make our lives a living hell.

Many teachers believe in contacting the family right away to report any infractions. If you know there are cooperative parents at home, of course it may be a good idea. But what about those students whose parents will deal with your call in a manner that may make things worse? Or the parents who are ineffectual? Sometimes it's a good idea to "strike a deal" with the perpetrator. After having a one-on-one (see One-on-One on page 50), I inform the student that it is appropriate for me to call his parents. When the student grovels and pleads and explains how he will be grounded for 7 years, I agree to *not* call if I have the student's word that he will at least make an effort to behave. (But don't make him promise to *never* misbehave. See Never Demand a Promise on page 57.)

Many times it really works because your students believe you are on their side. A point I must stress here: If it is something serious, you must inform the parents. If a child has missed ten homework assignments, the parents need to know about it, whereas the two of you can probably negotiate about one or two missed assignments. But do not leave yourself open to a parent who says you didn't tell him his son was in danger of failing or his daughter was truant. That is serious stuff.

Tons of Quizzes

For some courses, I do not give big midterms and final exams. Instead, I give many small quizzes—let's say 15 during the term. At the end, I tell them I will take the 12 highest grades and average them. It nullifies the few times a student may have been unprepared or just didn't do well. If a student misses three exams, however, there are no low scores to discount because I will count 12 grades.

This is a fair way of grading and rewarding good attendance, but it does involve a little more work for the teacher. I have found that some kids panic when everything hinges on one exam, and if I have only a couple of tests to go by, I really don't get an accurate overall picture of my students.

However, you would be remiss if you didn't assign the occasional heavily weighted project, because the reality is that the real world has stressful tests like SATs and reading placement exams.

Offer Choices

This Ginott strategy works extremely well with young children. If the class seems restless and you know they need a change, let them be the ones to decide what the change will be—sort of!

When you sense, for example, that they are growing tired of arithmetic problem solving, ask them if they would like to do something else. After that hurtful, resounding *"Yes!"* tell them they may choose either a spelling bee or a drawing lesson. What they do not have to know is that you were planning to teach these lessons all along. Giving them a choice makes them feel empowered. And you get to do what you had planned to do anyway.

Confer for Grades

At the end of each grading period, I have an individual conference with each student. It is usually done during an independent reading time. I first ask them to write down what grade they think they deserve and an explanation of what they did (or didn't do) to deserve it. Around 8 out of 10 students are usually right on target.

I think it is a wonderful opportunity on the students' part to try to convince you that they deserve a higher grade—and in some cases they do. How empowering to stand up for oneself! On the flip side, it is a lesson in humility for the truant who feels worthy of an A. It is a good opportunity to discuss frequent absences, missed assignments, and the effect the behavior has on his overall performance.

Finally, there are those students who have a 90 average but will ask for an 80. Such students must be taught to believe themselves worthy. One of my favorite students, Elena, had a 96 average and asked for a 75. I asked her to please convince me why I should lower her grade. I believe modesty prevented her from asking for her rightful due, so I had to point out the potential consequences of her false modesty. (Oh, by the way, she got the A because she couldn't convince me she deserved a C.)

"Class"—The Collective Noun

When a student is misbehaving, it is unfair to make the entire class stay after school. Yet sometimes a class has to work as one unit, as a *collective noun*, "a class."

I will often tell a class that they will go home as soon as everyone is quiet. If Scott feels like giggling, it is up to the class to let him know he is preventing the rest of them from going home. The class also has to learn to do this in a noncombative way—no "Shut up, stupid!" is allowed. Here is where the skill of not giving tacit approval comes in (see Tacit Approval on page 33). It's also your opportunity to give a quick grammar lesson on the definition of a collective noun.

Independent Reading, With Twinkies!

Romy, a student teacher of mine, suggested that the whole class read independently at the same time. Because it was a particularly hard-to-handle class, I told her that I thought it would take them forever to settle down. But we managed to refine a strategy that would actually quiet them down somewhat painlessly.

We all went to the library and chose a book. I let them choose any fiction book they wanted to read that was within their reading-level range. They were told that if they were not enjoying the book, they had to put it back and choose something else. I did not want them to read anything they weren't enjoying because I wanted reading to be fun for them. I would let them sit anywhere in the room. Many curled up in the doorway, some sat under desks, and some just moved into a quiet corner.

Now, what would make this reading lesson perfect? *Junk food!* So I would then bring out cookies and pass them out to the kids. Eventually, we had the cafeteria bring milk to drink with the cookies and other assorted gourmet snacks, such as Twinkies! (If you want to be a really nice person, you might give them a sugar-free snack, so those teachers who get them next period will not say terrible things about you!)

Go With the Roll

You planned this wonderful lesson on the history of the Pony Express and you know it is going to wow them. But something happened along the way and suddenly the class is deeply involved in a discussion on the concentration camp at Treblinka. You have no idea how the discussion got *there*, but it is fascinating. The kids are sharing feelings, ideas, and incredible insights. Should you get them back on track? Not if you don't have to. You know they will be dealing with the Holocaust in the future, so stick with something that has magic today. Of course, you cannot always do that because of curriculum demands, so you have to use your judgment. Learning isn't always about lesson plans.

Role Reversal/Role-Playing Technique

This is a wonderful strategy to make students look at themselves through your eyes, *and vice versa!*

When there is a problem in the class, try to role-play. Create a situation like the one you want explored, and ask for volunteers to be your cast of characters. You will learn that their insights usually help provide a refreshing, different perspective.

Let the kids know that you are stumped about how to handle a certain problem in the classroom. Ask someone to "be you," and you play the part of a student in the class.

You can use a role-play or a role reversal—either one is effective. The best part of this strategy is that it usually has a light-hearted quality to it and people laugh at what could otherwise be an unpleasant situation.

Am I Boring?

I did not use this tactic too often, but when you know your audience (see Chapter 13, Knowing Your Audience), this can be really fun and, more importantly, helpful to you as a teacher. This strategy stems back to a time when I was very insecure in a subject I was teaching. I was an English teacher at the time, but my principal threw in some history classes for me to teach. As a student, I had *hated* history with a passion because my history teachers seemed incredibly dry and boring. I suddenly had to teach about Ancient Greece, and all I knew about it was that it was old!

I crammed up on my history and was desperate to have my students enjoy the subject and not be "historically challenged" as I was. As I went along, I asked the class to let me know if I was losing them or turning them off. The best part is that I now love discussing Ancient Greece, and I like to think my students are discussing it as we speak.

Don't be afraid to ask the class if they are getting confused because it is better to know than to keep on repeating a sleep-inducing lesson.

A Fun Way to Limit Slang

Many times, teachers try to talk like the kids so that there will be no doubt that their teacher is "cool." But more often than not, the teacher sounds ridiculous to the kids, as well as patronizing. No one is impressed by a 55-year-old teacher in orthopedic shoes who says, "Yo, dude, you ain't done no work." As a matter of fact, slang does not belong in the classroom. In the streets, students are free to say whatever they choose, but in my room they are going to sound educated, because the reality is that people often judge us by how we speak. I want my kids to sound as smart as I know they are. To do that they must first be aware that they are using slang or nonstandard English. Rather than correct them each time they use a slang word, I put the class in charge of eliminating the word. For example, if anyone says *ain't*, the class points and says, "Lowden will kill you." The "ain't-sayer" has to smile and say, "Thank you." The kids really have fun with this, because it is said good-humoredly.

We all had a good laugh when Babs was corrected. She indignantly looked at the class and said, "I ain't say *ain't*." She had no choice but to laugh and realize that she had been totally unaware of her repeated use of the word.

A note here: Be careful not to devalue slang, which can be very colorful and cultural, but rather have your students know how to differentiate and use language appropriately.

Don't Overcorrect

The previous strategy is one we don't want to abuse. If we keep correcting every grammatical atrocity, then students learn to correct none. That is why I will just tackle one—for instance, "ain't" as I just described. Once they hear the error on their own, I'm onto a new one. "I seen" is a hot number in my school. Occasionally, I will let an "ain't" slip in while I am speaking to see if my class is on its toes. They love saying, "Lowden will kill you!" to Lowden herself (as I meekly mumble, "Thank you").

Student Revenge: Your Personal Evaluation

I call this "payback time." At the end of the year, I ask my students to evaluate the class they took with me—to tell me if they liked it and why, what I could have done to make it better, and what they liked best and least. It is up to you to include what you want to find out from them. They do not have to put their names on the papers, and I allow them the freedom to make comments. I stress that they should be as constructive as possible and should not be mean-spirited. (With a smile on my face, I do threaten to hire a handwriting analyst if anyone's comments are real mean!)

This is a good way for you to determine what has worked and what hasn't. My favorite response was from a student who wrote, "I love your class because you are so funny—well, at least you try to be and we kids get a kick out of that!" *Try* to be?

"Help! *I'm* Being Observed"

The moment you dread is getting closer. Your supervisor is going to come to your room armed with pen and paper to observe you, and you're sure your lesson will fall flat while your students are running around the room acting out the definition of "riot."

Don't worry—that rarely happens. Some teachers explain to the students that there will be a visitor to watch *them.* I always told them that the visitor was there to watch how I teach and how we interact. I tell them that it is a very important time for me and that I am counting on them to help me. I am always amazed at how supportive the kids are.

One year, I explained to the class that their enthusiasm would be helpful, and I encouraged them not to sit there dumbstruck. I did an experiment in science, and what followed made me cringe with embarrassment. Each child passed my principal and said in a less-than-subtle, loud voice, "Wasn't that interesting?" or "Wow!" It looked totally staged, but fortunately he didn't see it, which to this day still amazes me. Knowing you have a class on your side makes the observation nearly painless.

7

Setting Consequences

Every Act Has a Consequence

Now that the rules have been defined, it is a good idea to empower your students by having them help you determine penalties. One of my mantras is "Every act has a consequence." I cannot tell you how important it is to stress this, to convey the significance of individual responsibility.

Never give them ammunition to accuse you of being unfair. I always ask my students what they feel would be appropriate consequences in a given situation. Believe it or not, they are more strict than I would ever dream of being. Once, after a serious fight in which I was accidentally pushed, I asked the two participants what they believed would be a fair punishment. One boy suggested a month's detention, and the other offered to wash my car. Both punishments were inappropriate. A mere 2 days of detention was more than enough, as 2 days to them is an eternity.

Remember to stress that consequences can also be positive.

Rewards

It is so easy to punish, and it is also so negative. When a student works well, let him know that there are positive consequences. You can decide what the reward will be. It may be a token gift (I have given out pencils that I had personalized with the message "Great

Job") or a special privilege. If your classes are small enough, you can involve the parents in this and let them offer a reward at home.

Another thing I suggest is a class trip. Rather than exclude those students that I felt could not be trusted to go, I would announce the names of those who had earned the privilege to go. Instead of making the decision punitive to some, I would make the trip a reward for most.

Homework Penalty (With Room for Redemption)

Homework is the responsibility of the student, plain and simple. In most cases they have a choice whether to do it or not. If a homework assignment is not done, they get a –2. At the end of the term when we confer (see Confer for Grades on page 37), I add up all the minuses and deduct them from the student's grade average. Often, they may fail my class even though they passed exams.

Before you call me heartless, read on. I allow them to make up the missing homework within a short period of time—let's say 2 days. When they make it up, I give them back 1½ points. Now they only lose half a point, which may not add up to very much, but this still teaches them that there is a consequence.

Start With a 99%

This strategy can only be done in a class in which testing is not necessary, such as my sex education class. In such a class, dialoguing with me and with one another is the top priority. Yes, they will get tested, but those exams are more for me to evaluate what they are learning rather than to determine grades.

What I do here is give them a responsibility (because, in that class, personal responsibility is of utmost importance). I tell them on Day 1 that their final grade will be a 99%. They look at me in stunned disbelief. Then I add the conditional *however*. They are told to bring their journals for me to read and respond to each week, and that this is all they have to do for the term. If they fail to do that, I will take off 10 points from the 99 for each week missed.

I cannot tell you how happy they are just knowing they've secured a sure 99%. I also cannot tell you how many fail! It is a simple task, and if they cannot do it, they have to deal with the consequences.

I rarely allow them to bring it in the next day if they had forgotten it the previous day (although one year I was generous and gave them back 5 points the next day). Of course, absentees have to bring it in on the very day they return.

I truly believe this strategy helps develop a sense of responsibility. The rules are laid out, and you cannot be accused of being unfair.

The Tardy Quiz

A colleague of mine used to give an occasional "tardy quiz," a quick little test at the beginning of class. I would know she was giving it by the one or two kids camped outside her door after the late bell had rung. If students got to class late, the door would be locked and the latecomers got a 0 on the quiz. Her students never knew when she was going to spring her quiz, and it sure got them to her class on time.

Torture Sheets

My classes always loved this. When I would give a spelling test, I would have each student correct someone else's paper. The corrector would have to write his or her name on the bottom of the paper so that I would know who did the correcting.

Next, I'd write the correctly spelled words on the blackboard, and as we went over each word, students would look for any misspellings and make the necessary corrections. They would then bring the corrected papers to my desk, where I would quickly go over them. If they overlooked a misspelled word, or if they didn't correct it properly, they got a "torture sheet"—a piece of scrap paper on which they would have to write the misspelled word 10 times. They'd moan and groan, and I would smile.

When a paper had no errors on it, I would feign disappointment. It is a lot of fun, and the "game" is to make Ms. Lowden sad by not letting her give them a torture sheet. Of course, the bottom line is that they are real careful to make sure they make no mistakes.

You Are Not the Supply Store

There are students who choose not to bring a pen or pencil to school and who always seem to be out of notebook paper. Their rulers and other necessary school supplies are always missing. The easy way out is to hand these kids pens, paper, and so forth. *Don't!* That is not your job. They may end up not doing work because they have nothing to write with or on. Well, that is a consequence of not being prepared.

Before you think I'm too stingy or harsh, I have to stress again that you must know your audience. If his pen runs out of ink or if she has no more paper because she just used her last sheet, that is a different story. But even that has to have a small consequence, and so I suggest the next hint.

Collateral, Please

Before I lend a student a pen, pencil, ruler, or some other such supply, I ask for collateral. I have gotten earrings, keys, dimes, bus passes, wallets, and hats. At the end of the class, they return what they borrowed and I return their collateral.

I stopped taking keys because once a girl forgot to return my pen, I still had her key, and she was locked out of her house. But small tokens as collateral reinforce that we don't get things for nothing, nor should one expect that. I will admit that I have amassed at least $1.30 and a Knicks hat during my career. Who says teachers are underpaid?

When to Call Home

As a teacher, my best suggestion is for you to call home when you think you should. Your gut feelings are usually what you should trust, as well as your philosophic beliefs. However, there are times you *must* call home. When a student is in danger of failing your class, when she is consistently not doing her work, when he is not showing up for class, when one's behavior is out of character, or if you fear a student is in any kind of danger, you must make that call. Often during adolescence, drugs and alcohol rear their ugly heads, and it is important for you learn to see the signs.

SHOWING YOU'RE
ON THE SAME TEAM

In this section, I have included my favorite strategies for creating a comfortable classroom and reinforcing the concept that you and your students are on the same side. For a classroom to be comfortable, we must all feel safe. Our students have to deal with teachers, parents, and other students; they have to go out into the world and meet challenges. As a teacher, I give them "Lowden's Life's Lessons," which I will explain in more depth later in this chapter. Basically, they are suggestions to help get through life a little more easily. Whether or not they choose to follow them is completely up to the students.

In my classes, we share so much. Students are so open—not because I am so wonderful, but because I am not their parent! I do not judge them, and I don't have the power to cut off their allowances or telephone privileges. I am safe for them, and you should be, too!

8

Communicating Like a Pro

Acknowledge Feelings

Very often students, especially teenagers, will come to you with what feels to them like an earth-shattering problem. Many times the problems are serious, but most times they are really, in the whole scheme of things, not that terrible. Listen to them and acknowledge their feelings, but don't tell them they are silly to worry or that their "crisis" is not important. When I hear a student sobbing after a boy breaks up with her, I know her heart is breaking. She really believes it when she says she will never love anyone again and is going to run off to join a convent. It's easy to tell her there will be many more boyfriends and that this is just "puppy love." To this teen, her agony is *real*, and trivializing the situation is exactly what she does not want. Acknowledge her feelings and tell her that even though you know it is painful, you also know that she will survive, and that you'll be there if she needs to talk to you.

Never Deny Perception

I remember once when my daughter came home complaining that her teacher picked on her and no one else. My knee-jerk response was to say, "Right, Felicia, only you!" But that would only serve to alienate her more and put her on the defensive. So instead I said, "It must feel terrible to feel your teacher picks on you. Why do you think she does that?" She then believed I understood, and she was able to carry on a dialogue with me in which I could offer a bigger perspective.

I've said this before, but I will remind you again that our perception is our reality. Did you ever feel unloved by someone and they just laughed at you for being so silly? One doesn't need laughter, but rather someone to acknowledge what you are feeling and then be reassuring.

Use "I" Messages

I have been trained in conflict resolution, and one of the best strategies it uses is the "I" message. Basically, this means communicating your wants, needs, and concerns without attacking your student. Instead of saying, "You don't do a bit of work here and you're going to flunk," you might say, "I feel you're getting behind in your work and I'm concerned that I will not be able to pass you." I have even gone so far as to tell a student that I felt she disliked being in my class and asked if there was anything I could do to make our year together more enjoyable. Her behavior changed after that and to this day we keep in touch. I truly believe she didn't realize I had feelings and could be hurt. A high dose of honesty is strong cement.

"Let's" Instead of "You"

I can't stand when I visit my doctor and she says, "How are *we* today?" Likewise, I'm annoyed by the waiter who asks me, "Hi, what are *we* going to have to eat today?" But in the classroom, it is nice to include yourself as part of the group. It really supports the "same team" concept. "Let's take out our books" is nicer than "Take out your books." "What can *we* add to the story?" is more comfortable than "What can *you* add?"

Limit the "You Shoulds"

Recently when my daughter visited, I told her she should cut her hair, she should do a certain lesson with her class, she should . . . she should . . . she should. In her most tactful way, she suggested I try not using the phrase *you should* so much. She said that is something she became aware of when she began teaching. Rather than telling a student he should write something this way, my daughter would say, "Have you thought about writing it another way?" or "You might try it this way." This strategy empowers the student.

(By the way, I asked my daughter if she had "considered" a shorter hairstyle. It's *still* long. So much for that strategy!)

One-on-One

Embarrassing a student of any age by yelling at him can be pure agony. Asking a student to speak with you after class or after school, one-on-one, can result in miracles. The student has no audience to entertain, and you don't have to show how tough you are in front of an entire class. You can engage your students in conversation about things unrelated to school and air your grievance at the same time.

On occasion, I have even called a student at home. Very often, speaking on the telephone—an inanimate object—is a benign way to discuss the problem the two of you are having. Sometimes it works really well. Other times the phone lines scream with pregnant pauses. Prepare what you are going to say on the phone, but don't over-prepare because you have to listen and respond to what your student is saying. Your conversation depends as much upon your student's responses as on what you planned to say. Make sure you "know your audience" before you make the call.

How to Listen

Haven't we all seen a teacher holding a student captive with fingers waving in the air and a nonstop barrage of reprimands? With that we hear a meek little "But, but, but . . ." from the poor student who cannot get a word in edgewise.

I am sure we all agree that in all fairness we ought to listen to our students. I am not saying to give them equal time—even though I should—but at least give their point of view some respectful consideration. Here are a few strategies on how to listen.

While a student is talking to you, be conscious of your body language. You should be looking at him—not straightening your desk. A few "Uh-huhs" and a nodding head always help one feel that you are listening. In addition, you might pose a question about what he said.

Occasionally, a student would come to me with a pressing problem, and I would ask her to pull up a chair and sit next to or opposite me, preferably at a student's desk. Sitting at either side of the teacher's desk or standing while your student is seated is not conducive to comfortable communication.

Make Limits Total Rather Than Partial

We have to be careful with limits. Remember the old adage "Give 'em an inch and they'll take a mile"? There is a certain amount of truth to that. If your rule is that there will be no unexcused lateness without a consequence, then that is the rule. Don't allow them to wander in 3 or 4 minutes late after you've already set a rule.

I did not allow gum chewing. I would always get a request to allow gum chewing with the stipulation that if someone makes gum-chewing noises, then everyone has to spit it out. I once allowed myself to get talked into that. What a nightmare that became! I heard bubbles being popped, and when I said, "OK, no more gum," there was a chorus of protests with everyone pleading for one more chance. I learned my lesson because had I made the rule firm, I would not have had the confrontation at all. Remember, our goal is to avoid confrontation, and we do that by making ourselves clear.

My rule is not a partial rule, it is *the rule.*

State Rules Impersonally

By stating rules impersonally, you are focusing on the rule and not the child. I get upset when I hear teachers say things like "What's wrong with you? Can't you follow the rules?" How can we expect someone not to react defensively?

However, it is totally nonconfrontational when we just remind a child who is wearing a hat in your class that the rule is "No hats allowed." Period! End of argument! (Even better—no argument!)

Describe What You See (or Don't See)

To avoid confrontation, we know not to call our students *lazy, careless,* or *bad.* What we do instead is describe what we see without passing judgment. "Janet, I only see one page done when there were supposed to be three." Or, "Allen, I don't see the assignment you were supposed to complete." Calling students names will only elicit a defensive reaction. Merely state what you see and avoid confrontation.

Stay Simple: One Word or Sentence Will Do

Oh, let's save us all some breath. Have you ever found yourself explaining in great detail why a student must do homework? It becomes one of those boring lectures we all hated when we got them from our parents and our teachers. Now we are doing the same thing. Catch yourself when you do that and just state what you want—period!

A colleague of mine had a party and one of the girls left potato chips in her desk. He told her about the cockroaches the food would attract and what bad health habits she was developing and so on. She came to me and said, "I just wish he would've told me to throw away the potato chips—I would have done it in a second. I didn't even realize I had left them there."

Would You Talk to an Adult That Way?

I often hear teachers speaking to young people as though they were inferior beings. If you hear yourself criticizing a student, ask yourself if you would talk to an adult that way. Yes, I know they are not adults, but you would be a lot more sensitive to a peer. Why not be sensitive to your student?

Don't Futurize

When your third-grade pupil comes to school an hour late, don't remind him that he will never get a good job, because he couldn't care less. Trust me, he's not looking for employment and so your forewarning means nothing.

When I teach my ninth-grade students about the horrendous consequences of AIDS, it isn't real to them because at 15 you don't believe you can die. However, when I graphically describe the physical effects of STDs, they swear off sex for life!

When I tell a fifth-grade student she will not get into college because of her bad study habits, she too couldn't care less. She is still anxious about junior high!

So instead, make the consequences immediate. Make their future *tomorrow*. "If you enter my classroom late today, you will stay after school tomorrow." *That* is real to students.

Paraphrase

This is another popular strategy used in conflict resolution. Just paraphrase what you heard. When a student accuses you of being inhumanly unfair, repeat what you believe he said. You might say, "So you are saying that I am unfair because I expect too much from you?" The student is then hearing the words from you and can digest them more easily and address the issue. How many times have we said something that, when paraphrased back to us, sounds different?

Don't Mix Criticism With Praise

I remember one night I made this delicious meal. My husband was effusive with praise, and I felt wonderful until he said, "If only you were neater in the kitchen." There went the compliment . . . I was a good cook but a real slob.

In the classroom, we have to try to give unconditional compliments. Think about how often we say, "This is such good work, it just proves that if you stop fooling around, you can do so much." Wouldn't it be nicer to simply convey what great work the student has just produced? I am sure he knows all about his deficiencies, so why remind him in his moment of glory?

@#$%&* Yes or No?

As for cursing, I rarely allow it and only if it is appropriate. In my course on prejudice, for example, if a student is sharing a personal experience and an inappropriate word slips out, I let it go so as not to kill the effect or the mood.

Of course, this is up to you. Students will often slip and apologize to me. I ask them to apologize to everyone. I want them to know that inappropriate cursing is an affront to everyone, not just the teacher. The same rule goes for burping. For some unknown reason, burping is hysterically funny to the "burper"—and usually to no one else.

Forced Apologies Not Accepted

Many teachers believe they are instilling responsibility in young-sters by forcing them to apologize to someone to whom they believe an apology is owed. How many times have I seen a teacher or administrator dragging bodily an unwilling "atoner"? "Barbara, say you're sorry to Ms. Lowden *now!*" Barbara looks at my shoes and mutters those assigned words.

Everyone is surprised when I do not accept the apology at that moment. I stop Barbara in midsentence and tell her she can apologize if she thinks she should—at a time when it is sincere. I have offered kids the opportunity to write about what happened and if they think the situation was unfair they can express it—or they can do nothing at all.

To me, a coerced apology has as much value as a coerced confession and often liberates the apologist from real consequences.

The Double Message

I had no idea this was a strategy until my student teacher Jack told me how much he loved it.

One day, I was very angry at a girl, but while I was expressing my discontent, my hand was on her shoulder. I guess I was telling her verbally what angered me, as my hand on her shoulder was subconsciously telling her we were friends. If you are uncomfortable touching a student (see To Touch or Not to Touch on page 19), you can say something conciliatory that may make you both feel better. A gentle smile or wink can also alleviate a tense situation. Remember, a grudge helps no one.

What Would Another Teacher Tell Me?

Very often a student will come into the room accusing some teacher of being unfair, prejudiced, immoral, and sadistic. After talking to the student and using such strategies as paraphrasing and acknowledging feelings, you still have to calm this child down and find out if the allegations are exaggerated. (See Confronting Other Teachers on page 105.)

I remember Danny coming into my room, accusing Ms. Noam of hating boys. He told me that she always picked on boys and treated girls as if they were better. I then asked, "What would Ms. Noam tell me if I asked her about this incident?" He proceeded to tell me she would complain that he never does his homework and throws things around the room. Got the picture?

Conflict Resolution

Conflict resolution and peer mediation are two programs being implemented in schools all over the country, in which teachers, students, and parents go through a training program for several days. The result is that students are empowered to help other students settle disputes. A teacher is present, but two trained student mediators work with two (or more) disputants to prevent disagreements from escalating. They use many of the strategies mentioned here, using rules agreed upon before the mediation session. If your school does not have such a program, I suggest you encourage them to implement one.

9

Being Fair

Admit When You Are Wrong

Believe it or not, once in a while a teacher is wrong. Not me, of course, but others—yes.

Seriously, when you make a mistake, admit it. Too many people think it is a sign of weakness to make such an admission. To me, it is a sign not only of strength but of fairness.

I remember once pushing a very difficult student too far. I got him so angry he stormed out of the room and later opened the door and threatened me. The dean heard him and was going to suspend him. I asked if my student and I could talk privately. I admitted to him that I may have pushed too far, and he meekly said, "Maybe I overreacted." I said I wouldn't call his home, but he had to assure me he would be indebted to me for the rest of his life, to which he eagerly agreed. (Humor lightens everything!) He became more responsible in my class, and I was one the few teachers who had no subsequent confrontations with him.

Admit When You Don't Know Something

It took me many years to learn that many of my teachers did not know all the answers. They did what I call "the dirty trick," whereby a student asks a question to which the teacher does not know the answer, and the teacher says, "Good question. Why don't you research it and give us the answer?" Now, that is really dishonest!

Tell the children you do not know the answer but you would appreciate it if someone would research it. If no one volunteers, you should research it yourself or assign it for extra credit. No one knows everything, not even teachers—even though we sometimes behave as though we do!

Never Break a Promise

The broken promise is similar to the empty threat. The difference is that the broken promise leads not only to a lack of credibility but also to disappointment. If you break a promise, then the "It's not fair" refrain is totally justified. Our students hold us to our word—as they should.

When you make a promise, cover all your bases. I remember promising a third-grade class a trip to the playground as a reward for a job well done. I did not check the weather report and offered no alternative plan in case of inclement weather. You guessed it: The day we were supposed to go to the playground was a nasty, rainy day. So as a rational human being, I promised them we could go the *next* day. In unbearable wailing unison, they explained to me, "But you promised. . . ."

You know, it's not that bad sitting on a swing in the park when it's raining!

Never Demand a Promise

Do you think you might be tempted to sell your soul in exchange for that winning $10 million lottery ticket? Well, asking a student to promise that he or she will never call out again in order to avoid detention is the equivalent of the lottery ticket. Remember, he may even mean it when he makes the promise, but we all know about good intentions.

Try simply asking your student to make an effort not to call out, because making him swear on everything sacred usually doesn't work.

"I'm in a Bad Mood"

Whether you partied too much the night before, or your wife told you she's leaving, or you're just in a foul mood, you should warn your students. I have come to school with a very heavy heart and the last thing I felt like doing was teaching five classes, but part of the job description says I have to do just that.

One of the most difficult things is *not* to take your mood out on your students. So be fair and warn them. I have told my students I am in a sad mood and would appreciate it if they would help me by being cooperative. Kids are so amazing. They would usually jump on any student who misbehaved. (Be sure and let your kids know it's okay for them to ask for help if they're having a bad day, too.)

I resisted the urge to tell them I was sad every day—think I would lose some credibility?

"This Hurts Me More Than It Hurts You"

Remember when your parent said "This hurts me more than it hurts you!" as you were being disciplined? I never really bought that line until I became a teacher. In dealing with misbehaving students, I have had to demonstrate consistency and firmness, and that has often entailed doing things I didn't want to do. Teachers must be skillful enough to convey that punishing *really* is not what we want to do.

I remember planning an exciting class trip to the zoo. It was going to be a reward for the class if they behaved in a manner we had all agreed to. But this particular group tormented every teacher who crossed its path, and I was faced with the question of how I could take them to the zoo. The problem was doubly challenging because *I* wanted to go to the zoo. I could have taken the easy way out and offered them one more chance, a "deal" whereby they could make up for their misbehavior and still go on the trip, and we would all be happy, especially *me!* But I couldn't do it because (a) they had not lived up to their part of the bargain, (b) they had betrayed my trust, and more importantly, (c) they had been disrespectful to other teachers and it would be a slap in the face to my colleagues if my class was rewarded for its poor behavior.

A few months later, after much improved behavior, we went to the zoo and it was truly a trip they had earned.

No "Boys Will Be Boys"

In my lessons on prejudice awareness, I talk about acknowledged and unacknowledged prejudice. We all acknowledge racism as a horrendous thing, as we should. We also spend money for programs to halt this bigotry, as we should. But we seldom get upset about sexism because we don't even realize we are perpetuating it. I have seen boys get away with things we would never tolerate in girls. How upset we get when a girl hands in sloppy work, even though many of us do not hold boys to that same standard. And when a girl curses, we automatically tell her she is not being ladylike, whereas we will tell a boy who curses he is not being gentlemanly only if there is a girl present. No one should curse—period!

In all fairness, we should not minimize the behavior of a girl who hits a boy. We should not give girls the domestic chores and boys the executive and physical ones. Boys and girls should be able to interchange roles to have more equal classrooms and a more equal society. (See also Interchange Gender Pronouns on page 13 and Division of Labor on page 30.)

Etiquette Pitfalls

Did you think for a second I was going to tell you to teach the boys the "ladies-first" rule? Not on your life! Before you start telling me about tradition, I am going to tell you about treating all humans with kindness and respect. Good manners should be taught to all and if they are gender based, they are sexist. Why can't a person hold the door for whomever follows?

Please and Thank You

I find that people don't say "please" and "thank you" enough, and, as a result, neither do our children. If you, the role model, use them often and encourage children to do the same, maybe we'll all get into the habit of being polite. I remember buying cookies and offering each student one as I walked around the room while they read. Not one student said thank you. I had to stop a wonderful silent reading period to point it out. They were sure they had thanked me, but no one had. The next time they nearly kissed me for the cookies. Making them aware was important because individuals often think they are very polite when in fact they may even be rude—and that applies to us, the teachers, as well.

Gauge the Amount of Homework

The teacher at the elementary level, or in the self-contained classroom, should be careful not to assign too much homework. Overload often leads students to accept the consequences rather than do the work. Be fair, and you can even be kind by occasionally giving them the "night off."

In the secondary schools, where the subjects are departmentalized, students often end up with five projects at the same time. Confer with your colleagues and impress upon your students that you need to be told when they are being overloaded with work. But beware the student who considers five math problems overload!

10

Bonding Strategies

The Sanctuary

This strategy is a powerful one. I explain to my students that my classroom is a sanctuary. They must define the word ("a safe place"). Then we brainstorm answers to the question "What makes a classroom safe?" The resulting list is put on the bulletin board and must be respected. When someone hurts someone else's feelings, I stop immediately and ask, "What is this classroom called?" They will say, "It is a sanctuary." I keep doing this until they pick it up and say to each other, "Hey, quiet! This is a sanctuary." I never thought it would take effect as well as it did, but the students valued the safe feeling they had in the room. At first it was a joke, but then it became a source of comfort. Children who in the past would never read aloud would do so now, because they knew no one would make fun of them if they made a mistake. (See also Tacit Approval on page 33.)

"I'm on Your Side"

This is a strategy I picked up when my husband and then-teenage daughter were having an argument. I think it was over something life-shattering, like the stereo was too loud.

With great exasperation, I heard him say, "Felicia, I'm on your side. I am your biggest fan." It really rang true because it *was* true. As a teacher, your students have to understand that you are on their side, and the best way to do that is to tell them.

After I assure them I am on their side, I explain why. "If you do well, I look good. If I have to fail you, I look bad!" In my course on prejudice, we learn that there is always an "us" and a "them." You have to establish that you are all on the same team and make it clear that you are an ally—not an adversary.

Being Vulnerable: Share a Giggle

Sometimes we think we have to be the stalwart teacher, never letting our guard down, never being vulnerable. Being human is a wonderful quality and we're even born with it. Every now and then let your students know you can take a joke, and laugh at yourself.

Once I walked into my classroom and noticed an air of excitement that was almost out of control. I wanted to believe it was because they were about to learn how to parse a sentence, but just then I noticed a whoopee cushion ready to be sat on by me! I had two choices: One was to get angry, and the other was to be the butt of their joke (pun intended). I chose the latter and made them suffer a bit before I plopped into my chair. It made the anticipated sound, and I just looked at them straight-faced and said, "Oh, my! Excuse me." They then knew I had seen it all along and we all had a great laugh. Again, I knew my audience and was able to be part of a joke. Perhaps with a different group I'd have seen it as a mean-spirited act and would have had a different response.

Relating Your Own Experiences

Many teachers keep their private lives just that—*private.* It certainly is one's right. I, on the other hand, find that by telling my kids little anecdotes about my life away from school, I actually become human in their eyes. (But don't overdo it. You could become a bore and lose the focus of your lesson.)

I will never forget a first grader expressing shock that I had a family. Another student giggled at the thought of my having a first name. To many students, we are teachers and that is our life. Kids always say, "Get a life," and by sharing some of your stories from beyond the four walls of your school, they may actually believe you have one.

Those Special Few Minutes

Be prepared, there are going to be some students who just rub you the wrong way. You just don't like them. They may whine, they may laugh too loudly, they may be show-offs, but in your heart of hearts, you feel shame for feeling the way you do. Don't! Your students certainly do not view all their teachers with equal admiration.

Even though it's natural and human to like some individuals more than others, one still has to refrain from playing favorites in any obvious way. The best way to make sure you don't show favoritism is to admit favoritism to yourself—and to no one else!

However, to ensure that I don't show favoritism, I occasionally put aside a couple of minutes to "kid around" with those students or make them feel special in some way. I may include them in spelling sentences or send them on a special errand. This strategy assuages my conscience for not being perfect and not enjoying every student with equal intensity.

15 Seconds of Fame

I like to give as many students as possible their 15 seconds of fame. What I do is "personalize" my spelling sentences and my handouts by including my students' names.

An example would be:

Circle the nouns in the following sentence: "Shep and Annie think Ms. Lowden is the greatest teacher who ever lived."

You usually hear chuckling as they do their work. Just try and make sure everyone is included at some time, and be careful not to be hurtful.

Creative Excuses

You all know how we say "The check is in the mail." What a boring and uncreative excuse for saying we forgot or that we're a little short this month.

Well, kids have *their* excuses, such as "I am late because the alarm clock didn't go off." The student knows (and I know) that she went back to sleep and pushed the snooze alarm 10 times too many. So I encourage my students to at least be creative and entertain me. I have had students attacked by a herd of wild bison while walking down Flatbush Avenue in Brooklyn, and I've heard about robbers who break into their homes late at night to steal the assignments they have so industriously worked to complete.

Have no fear, I still make them pay the consequences—only I do it laughing!

Bend the Rules

Oh, come on, stop being a meanie! You know the rules and so do they. They know you don't let them walk around the room—but it is 95°F in the room, they are bored to death, and they can't bear to hear about one more Roman numeral. Today the no-walking rule seems impossible to uphold. So cut the lesson short and let them walk around a bit or chat with a neighbor. Bending the rules once in a while does not mean you abdicate your authority in the classroom—it just demonstrates that you are flexible.

Journals

Keeping a journal can be applied to most subjects. I have found them useful as an avenue for children and teens to express themselves emotionally, as well as creatively. I have communicated with students who needed someone to be a receptive ear for their self-exploration, through prose and sometimes through poetry. In my sex education class, they were able to ask me things in the privacy of their journals that they felt embarrassed about asking in front of the whole class. I write a response to everyone. As one girl said, "I love my journal. It's like having a diary that talks."

But you must be very careful with these. Remember, you are not a trained counselor and should not be dispensing therapy but rather having conversations with your students. You must tell them that the journals are strictly confidential and will be shared with no one *unless* you feel they are in danger. By law, you must report a situation that endangers a minor. I had a girl living among nine crack addicts and had to have her removed from the home. I have become aware of potential suicides, as well as sexually abused youngsters. I reported these cases and felt comfort in knowing they were rescued.

Be careful what you say. I always respond to the journal with the understanding that a parent may read it the second the child leaves the house. I usually try to say what I suspect the parents want to say but have difficulty communicating. For example, one boy complained that his father is always screaming at him. From his description, the father sounded like a royal pain, but of course I couldn't say that. I acknowledged his feelings, and then offered the following suggestion: "It must feel terrible to feel you are being yelled at all the time. Perhaps you might try writing your dad a letter expressing how you feel. Sometimes parents don't realize their children are struggling. Good luck!"

Know When You Are Overly Involved

Occasionally, a student will see you as a confidant, and it is up to you to learn how deeply to get involved and when to distance yourself.

I remember a dear student who would tell me her problems. I found myself spending too much time at home thinking about how I could help her. Some teachers live vicariously through their students, and they have to learn that when their favorite athlete doesn't get picked for the team, they shouldn't take it personally. The reality is that most students will distance themselves from you, but that rare student who needs to consume you has to be pushed back as gently as possible.

Read Aloud to Your Students

Anthony Alvarado, former New York City chancellor of schools, was our district superintendent. He was a brilliant educator who demonstrated a great lesson when he was an invited guest speaker at a monthly teacher conference. He came in to speak to us and instead took out a storybook and began to read to us. He read and read and, before long, we were all sitting there engrossed in the story.

We adult educators did everything but suck our thumbs and twirl our hair. He asked us to read to our students as often as possible. He was not talking only about little children, but about teenagers as well. It is one of the most bonding techniques a teacher can share with her students.

Celebrate Birthdays

Younger students love to have their birthdays acknowledged. Teens often pretend they don't care, but don't believe them for a minute. I suggest having a bulletin board with a list of everyone's birthdays so you can see at a glance whose birthday it is.

Don't forget to acknowledge those poor, deprived students whose birthdays fall on the holidays or during summer vacations. I'm still sore at my mother, who gave birth to me in July—depriving me of hearing my classmates sing "Happy Birthday" to me.

"I Thought of You"

Occasionally, I would see something in a newspaper or magazine that I thought would be of interest to a particular student. I would clip it out and deliver it either before or after the class met. Once I bought a ceramic turtle at a yard sale (for a big 50 cents) for a boy in my class who was fixated on turtles. You would think I had bought him a new Mercedes by the grin on his face. He could not believe I had bought it specially for him for no reason. He told me he would save it for the rest of his life. It has probably turned up at his own yard sale, but it served a wonderful purpose at the time. It made someone feel important.

Another feel-good strategy is to mail that newspaper or magazine article to a student's home. What child doesn't love to see an envelope personally handwritten and addressed to him or her—rather than to mom or dad?

Morning Meetings

This is a strategy used in the Friends School. In the morning, each child is free to share anything with the rest of the class. They usually make some kind of an announcement. Someone might mention that her Uncle Louie is coming from Oshkosh to visit, or another that his mother is having a baby. I have seen kids throw out a personal problem with which they needed help. They can relate a dream or merely a good laugh they had the night before. It is very bonding but usually works well only with a small group. It is up to you, the teacher, to make sure that everyone gets equal time. Beware: There is often that one student who wants to relate every detail of a 3-hour TV special.

Lowden's Life's Lessons (or, Teaching Winning Ways)

(Of course you can substitute your name for mine in this strategy, but it may not be as alliterative. This is my quick course in "Nicen Up 101"—the course title is from my students.)

Sharing secrets that will make your students more agreeable to other teachers is something they might benefit from more than anything you teach from a textbook. Here are a few examples:

- I tell my kids never to admit that they didn't study when they get a 100 on a test. (Let the teacher think they studied their heads off.)
- I suggest that on the first day of classes they sit near the teacher and not run to a hidden corner because that makes a poor first impression.
- I stress that being "in a teacher's face" only makes the teacher hostile to them, and it is the teacher who has the power.
- I remind them that being nice—or using honey instead of vinegar—works! It is hard to dislike someone who is pleasant and cooperative, but it is really easy to dislike that disrespect-ful student who mouths off at you.
- I encourage them to do some damage control after they've been disrespectful to a teacher. They can approach the teacher, admit they "lost it," and ask if they can start all over with tomorrow being the first day.
- I teach them to use a lot of the communication strategies I describe in this book. Most of the strategies are appropriate for all ages.

The Bellhop Bell

I loved my bell so much that I passed it on to my daughter, who has not quite had the nerve to use it yet. It is a bell just like the one you see on the desk of a hotel—you know, the one you ring to get attention. And that is exactly what I do!

I ask the kids not to move a muscle when they hear it. This becomes a game to them, and when they are still, I tell them how great they are and how much I love my bell. I then ask them in all seriousness to please be quiet when they hear the bell. As a reward, they will not have to endure my shrill shriek.

(Beware: There is always one student who begs to ring the bell and goes on a power trip and can't stop!)

Assure Students You Will
Tell Their Parents Something Wonderful

Many students go into cardiac arrest when parent–teacher conferences take place. Many of them know they are failing in school and dread the disapproval from their parents when they get home. It could be a terrifying moment, so to make everyone happy, I assure the students that I will find something wonderful to say about each and every one of them so that they don't get grounded for life. Every child has something special to be said about him or her—we just have to look a little further in some cases.

Thank Them for the Joy They Bring

You are going to have days that will make you thank your lucky star that you chose to be a teacher. You will be rewarded by seeing the light bulbs go on above their heads. Your students will tell you how they love you, and you will just have a great time. Why not share those good feelings with the very people who gave them to you by thanking them for the joy they brought you that day?

BUILDING CONFIDENCE
THROUGH EARNED PRAISE

When people feel good about themselves, they believe the sky's the limit. It is you and I who have to tap into those feelings of self-worth and facilitate growth. We have to help develop our students' belief in themselves before they can reach their full potential. Hopefully, some of these strategies will germinate the seeds of self-assurance.

11

Self-Esteem Strategies

Praise, Praise, Praise—But Don't Overpraise

Remember, if you are too effusive, your compliments become meaningless. Sincere praise can only make a student feel good, but it is crucial that you praise for efforts and accomplishments rather than looks. (Unless, that is, your student is all decked out for a special occasion.)

When students work well with one another, express appreciation for their ability to cooperate. When a child hands in a drawing, focus on something special in it, such as use of color, composition, or imagination. When a student cracks a truly funny joke, laugh. That, too, is a form of praise.

Sometimes, a teacher might tell a student who wrote a nice poem, "Wow. You are the greatest poet!" But, come on, little Melissa is not Keats and she probably knows it, and so she may be uncomfortable with that compliment. However, telling her how beautiful her imagery is will likely be more meaningful and affirming.

Overpraising can have some real pitfalls. Giving too much praise and imposing expectations that are too high can be threatening to a student. The child who is told repeatedly, "You are always so good . . . I wish everyone was like you!" or "I know you will never disappoint me" can be overwhelmed and feel unfairly burdened. All children will at some time disappoint you; don't expect that even your star pupils will always be perfect.

Acknowledge Improvements

One of the things we as educators occasionally forget is to acknowledge improvements, no matter how small. A little acknowledgment can go a long way toward raising self-esteem and getting the results you and your students desire. Notice how often we will call home to tell a parent that Judy isn't doing her homework. But do we call home when Judy starts to do her homework on a more regular basis? Usually not, because homework being done on time should be expected.

But *soften up,* and acknowledge that the improvement in her habits is not going unnoticed.

Enthusiastic Credit When Credit Is Due

In class, when someone contributes something truly wonderful, let him or her know.

I had a colleague, Deborah, who, after I gave her a suggestion, would say, "Renee, that was a *fantastic* idea." I remember feeling a little surprised by her great effusion. And something else was going on. Her enthusiasm made me feel as though my ideas were second only to Einstein's. Her praise made me feel wonderful, so I started being more enthusiastic when my students came up with fine ideas of their own. Their glowing faces indicated that they were also believing in the value of their own ideas. Not a bad way to feel!

Remember that some students may be embarrassed, so tell them after class how impressed you were by them. Just be careful never to be patronizing or insincere. Here is a case where you must know your audience and be selective—and don't overpraise. The idea must really be exceptional.

Put-Ups, Not Put-Downs

"If you have nothing nice to say, say nothing." This wisdom comes from my father (and probably yours, too).

Worthy compliments only make people feel good. Put-downs hurt, even when the child says, "Words won't hurt me." You may be relieved when a student who is being picked on says, "I don't care."

But don't believe the child for a second, because words not only can hurt, they can leave scars.

Don't Rush to Correct

Remember when you were a child and you stood up cheerfully to give your interpretation of an answer you just knew the teacher wanted? And then the teacher said, "Wrong. Sit down. Who can give me the right answer?" Can you remember how your face stung with embarrassment?

What *I* say is, "That's not quite what I had in mind, but that's an interesting way to look at it" or "That was a good guess." Simply dismissing an incorrect answer can intimidate the child and discourage him or her from volunteering an answer in the future for fear of being humiliated.

Call Home for the "Average" Student

There are students who always do average work. They are neither Madam Curies nor Charles Mansons. They are just average students who come to school and do their work.

Notice how those who do well earn praise and high grades and acknowledgment, and those who misbehave earn a telephone call to their parents. Well, every once in a while, I call the home of a student who puts in great effort. I will tell the parent how I enjoy his child and what a pleasure it is to have her in my class. The parent usually asks, "OK, what's wrong?" After I assure him that that was my only motive, I usually have a beaming parent and the next day a beaming student. Everyone profits from this—and it only takes a couple of minutes of my time.

"I Knew You Could Do It" (and More)

"I knew you could do it" is a wonderful thing to hear, but sometimes it's not enough. Not too long ago, I was asked to give a speech to a large professional group. I get terribly nervous speaking before a large audience, and so for a while I was turning down those engagements. I finally decided I had to overcome this fear. I accepted an engagement and prepared (and worried) for a month. The big night came and it went just fine. When I came home and told my family all went well, they said, "We knew you could do it." What I really wanted to ask was, "Why did you think I could do it?" But that would be fishing for compliments, and modesty prevents that.

So when my students accomplish something they believed they couldn't do, I tell them *why* I knew they could. For instance, I had one girl who feared speaking aloud in front of the class, and I told her that I knew she could do it because she has so much to say and such a warm way of speaking.

A Little White Lie

I don't want you to read this book and walk away saying I told you to lie. However, a fib is different from a lie. OK, maybe it isn't, but sometimes we have to cross our fingers behind our backs to save a child from pain or embarrassment.

For instance, I once told a boy that I thought his haircut was nice when in fact it looked as if the barber had had one drink too many. If you are so honest that an untruth cannot escape your lips, try to give a noncommittal response like, "It sure is unique."

When I ask my husband if he thinks I am prettier than Michelle Pfeiffer, he says, "Renee, there's no contest!" or "What a silly question!" I take that as I want.

"You've Been Miseducated' "

Speaking of a little fib once in a while, here is an example of how it can raise the self-confidence of students.

I loathe tracking and ache for the students who are assigned to the "slow" track. It has to be humiliating to them. So I will tell my students that having read their records, I believe them to be underachievers. I explain that somewhere along the way, they were "miseducated," and in most cases that is the truth. I have had students believe they were capable of much more and—lo and behold!—they allow themselves to learn so much more. I have seen scores skyrocket and, more importantly, I have heard them tell others that they'd been "miseducated" and are more capable than others believe them to be.

Tracking

One of my principals used to give us lectures on why it was so important to raise the self-esteem of our students. At the same time, she had the school divided into "smart" classes and "not smart" classes. I don't care what euphemism one uses. By assigning the number 1 to the top class and 10 to the bottom class, you are defining these students to themselves and others. So I have to use the aforesaid "You've Been Miseducated' " strategy for these bottom groups.

The argument for tracking is, "All the students know who the smart kids are anyway." That is fine. No one complains about being too smart. That's why I have no objection to honors classes. But it is the middle and bottom classes that do not need to be publicly defined. Using a room number serves the same purpose. It defines a group without defining its abilities. Instead of 4-10, it would be 4-301.

One year a new teacher suggested we put students in Grades 7–9 in the same English class with all reading levels represented. I didn't think it would work but *Darn!* these new teachers are smart, so I went along with her plan. We were lucky enough that year to be involved in an experimental program and had about 18 students per class. As a result, we were able to grade each student according to his or her own abilities.

What we saw, amazingly, was that a student who had a low reading score might be very verbal and contribute as much to a discussion as a high scorer. The kids all helped one another and it was awesome. Most of you aren't lucky enough to have such small groups, but if you are, go ahead and try something like this. Our luck only lasted a year. The funding dried up and we were back to 30 per class, and a class such as the one I just described cannot work with such a huge academic and chronological gap.

Some of Us Can't Spell

Here I am, about to encourage you to have separate spelling groups. Remember, I'm the same person who loathes tracking, and you ask if I am really telling you to have two different groups? Yup. Some folks are simply terrible spellers, even though they excel in advanced calculus (and then there are people like me: I can spell, but need all my fingers to add up numbers!). I stress to my students that spelling has nothing to do with intelligence—that some of us are better spellers than others. I point out that Einstein was an allegedly horrendous speller, and he didn't do too badly! I then give my students the opportunity to choose a spelling group that they feel would be appropriate for their ability. I will ask, "Who is a so-so speller?" There is always a brave soul who will raise his hand, and then the rest follow suit. They know their spelling words will be a little easier, or that perhaps they will get fewer words to memorize. By openly discussing poor spelling skills, I destigmatize it, and those with trouble can focus in a more relaxed manner.

Wonderful Comments on Paper

Every student's heart skips a beat as the papers on which they worked so laboriously are being returned. What is the first thing they see from 20 yards away? *Red ink!* We all associate that color with criticism. But there is nothing that says criticism has to be all negative and that we cannot find something kind to say. Even when a paper has more red ink on it than black, you can tell a student that there are some really good ideas here or how much you are looking forward to the revision. Putting a happy face on the top of the paper is fine, but please scrap the frowning faces, unless that's what you want to see on your students' faces. You also might try using purple or green ink once in a while.

Post Every Student's Work

Many teachers believe that the "best" papers should be exhibited on the bulletin boards. But there are always those children who don't get 100%, or have terrible handwriting, or just produce average work. Those students never see their work up on the board, even though they have tried as hard as they could and worked to their full potential. As a teacher, I feel we should acknowledge all of our students, not only the ones who score high on tests. I put up papers at random (though I am careful not to post failing papers, or ones that would embarrass a student). Sometimes I will casually mention that I need papers to put up on the bulletin board, and if they would just drop their papers on my desk, I will hang them up. It always surprises me that the students who often do not do well drop their papers for me to exhibit. Everyone needs to be acknowledged, and this strategy demonstrates to me that they too want to be seen. I have seen students take extra pains to write as neatly as possible so their work will look good.

Often teachers will hang up papers riddled with errors. I still display these papers, but the bulletin board is labeled "Work in Progress." I want the student to recognize that his or her work is not finished merely because it is being displayed.

"I Got a 97%! What Did You Get?"

Have you noticed that it is only the students who get very high grades who yell across the room to another, "What did you get on the test?" Very seldom does a student with a failing paper do that.

I tell my students that they can tell their own grade, but they are not to ask about a classmate's grade in front of others. I assure them that if their friend has a good grade we will all know, and if not, silence will be enough. This is why I try to minimize competition for grades. (See also The Sanctuary on page 61.)

AVOIDING CONFRONTATION

To have a safe and comfortable classroom, you have to do everything possible to avoid confrontations. Remember, other than their parents, your students probably consider you the most unfair person in the world. Kids have these universal characteristics where they will roll their eyes and suck their teeth while muttering, "It's not fair!" So the following strategies have been designed to make your room as "unfair-proof" as possible. If you apply these techniques, I guarantee that you will have minimal discipline problems.

I have watched teachers stumble because they would not or could not respect the needs of their students. Too often teachers feel they must exercise *control* over their students at the expense of genuine *communication*. Some of us go on automatic and say things we shouldn't. Try to raise your consciousness so you will stop yourself before there is a confrontation. Let's make that classroom safe and fun!

12

Preventing Showdowns

Everything Is Embarrassing

Having taught teens throughout most of my career, I know with some certainty that to them, everything is embarrassing. A new haircut that didn't come out like the picture in the magazine is sheer agony. A pimple is almost as bad as being told one has a terminal disease. Younger children often panic at the very idea of having to get up in front a class to read. We all remember those moments. So be sensitive. Remember, embarrassing a student sets up a barrier between the two of you.

Humor, Not Sarcasm

OK, I know a kid sometimes needs a real put-down, but as teachers, we should not be the ones to do that. Sarcasm is hurtful, and the less sophisticated student misses the sarcasm and takes it as a put-down (which it actually is).

I once witnessed a colleague of mine say to a student, "Maybe if you had half a brain you would understand." When the student responded with curse words, the teacher was outraged and called home. Later, when the teacher asked me if I had heard the boy curse at him, I asked him if he would ever speak to me that way if I wasn't paying attention to him. Of course he wouldn't. Then why did he think it was OK to talk to his student that way?

I want to impress upon you that a good laugh is a great tension reliever. It also connects us as human beings. However, sarcasm and humor at someone else's expense are totally unacceptable and can be downright cruel.

The Biggest No-No: "Only Kidding"

I would rather my students use swear words than hurt someone's feelings and then say, "I was only kidding." That is not allowed in my room. "Only kidding" is one of the few things that infuriates me, and my students know it. We talk about ruthless honesty—calling someone "fat cow" is not said to make someone aware that he or she has a weight problem, but rather to be cruel and insensitive. I tell them that if they want to make a joke about someone, try some self-deprecating humor. It can be very funny—after all, Joan Rivers made a fortune doing it.

"Shut Up!"—*Not!*

I don't know if being told to shut up offends you as much as it does me. Try never to say "Shut up" to a student or a class. It's a demeaning and highly disrespectful expression. Asking someone to please be quiet or to calm down accomplishes the same thing without putting the student on the defensive.

"I Told You So"

Don't you just hate it when someone reminds you that he "told you so"? It seems we teachers can't wait to tell the student who we've reminded about something how we told them so.

"Didn't I tell you that you would lose your book?"
"Didn't I tell you that you would get into trouble hanging out with her?"
"I told you so. Now maybe you will listen to me."

Sound familiar? Kids respond unpleasantly to that, and it usually gets their eyes rolling. If you do that and they react negatively, I will have to say *"I told you so!"*

Avoid Arguments

Here's a painful reality of the life of a teacher: When you get into an argument with a student (other than one that's academic in nature, of course), *you* usually lose, even though it may appear that you won. When bickering with students, we lose some of our dignity in front of the class and find ourselves in the middle of a power struggle.

If the verbal haranguing goes on for more than a minute, I suggest you call a truce and have a one-on-one after class.

Choose Your Battles

Sometimes we just have to overlook a minor broken rule, and I stress *minor.* If you are a teacher who yells constantly about every major and minor infraction, your students stop hearing you after a while. In my classes, I did not yell often but, rather, used the hard stare, the smile, the "Excuse me," the lowering of my voice, and the other strategies mentioned earlier in the book (see Chapter 3). When nothing else worked, I found myself losing it (see Going on Automatic on page 10) and would become the irate teacher I had hated in the fifth grade. My kids would sit up, and I'd hear them whisper, "She really means it." Because I treated minor infractions lightly, my students took the rare display of anger quite seriously.

Don't forget, you can win the battle but lose the war. One of my students stopped coming to school because he was constantly being punished by most of his teachers for minor things, which I truly believed he could not help. So what was the result? He just stopped working.

Start All Over

Sometimes situations get so out of hand that there is irreparable damage. A student has said horrible things to you, and you don't think you will ever forgive her. You have violated every standard you set for yourself the day you became a teacher by trying to hurt her back.

After you cool off, you owe it to both of you to start all over. You might speak to the student after school, agree to a cease-fire, and go on as though nothing has happened. *Don't* rehash the incident that brought you to this point, because nothing will be accomplished and the hurt will only intensify. There is usually a little awkwardness for a day or two, but after that there is something of a secret bond there as well.

Beware of Empty Threats

We all know the teacher who screams, "I'm going to have you suspended" and "I'm going to call home" and so on. Then he cools down and does nothing. It may work once, but after a few times your students will catch on and you will lose your credibility. (If you follow the next strategy your credibility rating will soar.)

Pick a Rule and Stick to It (It's All in the Perception)

This is an invaluable strategy that has to do with perception. Too many times we resort to nasty, empty threats. I must admit that I am not guiltless here, but I've discovered a wonderful way to alter perception.

In order to set a standard, I choose the rule I hold most sacred— the one concerning unexcused latenesses, which I find intolerable— and always enforce it. Latecomers distract the class and show a disregard for all of us and toward the lesson in progress. I tell my students that I will gladly accept a late pass from a teacher, but if they choose to hang out instead of coming in on time, they will be penalized. I take off 1 point and there is nothing they can do to make up for the loss of this point. When we meet about their grades (see Confer for Grades on page 37), I then point out their latenesses, add up the minuses, and deduct them from the final grade.

I have had students who deserved a 70 for their grade, but had 15 points deducted for lateness. Needless to say, they failed and had no one to blame but themselves. Once they saw the tangible consequences of their latenesses, I earned a reputation as one who means what she says.

Once when I was teaching my sex education class, for which they all knew they could not be late, the bell was just about to ring when I heard Michael yelling to his friends. "I can't be late," he exclaimed, "I have sex with Lowden now!" Thank goodness that comment wasn't taken out of context! We had a good laugh, but Michael was on time!

Some students will just cut and hope you think they are absent. Warn them that lateness results in only 1 point off, but that the penalty for cutting is just short of capital punishment. Here I must stress the importance of keeping good attendance records.

No Spur-of-the-Moment Rules

Very often, a teacher will condemn behavior that was never defined as wrong, and, as a matter of fact, was usually tolerated. To a student, it feels as if you just made up the rule, and in some cases that may be just what you did. This is really unfair, and if you are called on it, you should let that particular infraction slide this one time but define it clearly to prevent it from happening again. A teacher with whom I once worked used to let the boys wear hats in the room (even though it was a school infraction). One day, a boy disrespected him, and he got the boy in trouble for wearing a hat. Now that's unfair!

To Chew or Not to Chew—That Is the Question

Your school may have the rule that gum is banned in class. If this is the case, the point is moot. However, if faced with the decision, there are two options: yes or no! The rule must be total, not partial. (See Make Limits Total Rather Than Partial on page 51.) Gum is often placed under the desk when the flavor is gone, and you don't win prizes with the custodian. I *never* let students chew gum because of a real-life trauma I experienced.

I was in the sixth grade, taking a reading test for grade placement. The girl behind me was cracking her gum. Instead of reading, I found myself counting her "gum clicks," and I ended up 2 years behind. I had to take the test over to be placed properly. So I tell my students this story and inform them they will have to carry the burden of my childhood. After the groaning stops, I stress that there may be a few noise-sensitive people in the room and they should not have to be distracted.

Set Up Winning Situations

This strategy can have a wonderfully positive effect on a class or student. One day, my daughter came home from school very energized. It was a new term, and she had asked the teacher to consider a clean slate for grades rather than the traditional cumulative approach, which would reflect grades from the beginning of the year. The teacher said, "I don't like your idea. Tell me why I should do what you suggest." Felicia, who was not usually outspoken, got into a lengthy debate with her and "convinced" her. The class cheered, and my daughter was the hero.

When I met with the teacher, I asked her if she had set up the situation. She winked and I knew. She said, "I hope Felicia has the confidence to always speak up for what she believes." She definitely made an impact on my daughter!

Don't Force Students to Lie

In my parent workshops, I hear parents force their children to lie and then accuse them of being liars.

For instance, a father gets a call from school about his son's truancy. The boy walks in and the father asks how school was. The son says, "Fine." The father is outraged at his lying son. The child lied to get out of deep trouble with his dad, but it was the father who was dishonest first. If he had been honest, he would have told his child about the phone call, but he chose to trap his son in a lie.

So, when you, the teacher, see a student where she shouldn't be, be up-front right away. Don't expect a student not to lie when forced into a corner. Haven't you ever complimented a woman on her hideous dress when asked if you liked it?

Make Rules Specific: Narrow Them Down

One of my pet peeves is when a school sets rules such as "Hitting a teacher is forbidden." To me that is a given. Is there one student who really thinks it is OK to raise a hand to a teacher? So why all the rules? But it does sound good to the parents and the rule makers if there are lots of rules.

The reality is that students seldom read the rules if there are too many. I like to eliminate rules that everyone knows are infractions and clarify those that are questionable. For instance, my school has a rule that says, "Every student is to dress appropriately for learning." What does that mean? Every child should wear a "thinking cap"? It needs to be spelled out. Perhaps it means no hats, no tank tops, no miniskirts. Only then will it be clear—and rules that are clear and specific will attract readers. We mustn't write rules that look like the standard contract we are asked to sign when we buy a new car.

No Sides

Two against one is never fair. Even if you agree with one student, as a teacher it is up to you to mediate a situation, not decide who is right. Of course, good judgment is required here. If one student is being abusive or threatening, you must intercede. But most arguments can be worked out, and often if you take sides, you end up being the bad one. I did it once, and with all my good intentions, ended up being accused of trying to break up a good friendship.

Time-Out

I talked about avoiding arguments, and again I stress how important that is. Sometimes, after you have tried every trick in the book, you may have to give a child (it is easier with younger students) a time-out. You might excuse her from continuing a lesson and allow her to put her head down on the desk until she is able to work. You might suggest she sit right outside the door until she cools off. Try and suggest this with compassion and not with anger. Sometimes we have to hone those acting skills that we, as teachers, all have.

Hurry! Shut Out the Lights

No, I am not talking about a video I am about to show. I am talking about an instant attention getter. I usually use this strategy when I feel I am losing control of a class or when a fight is about to erupt. I turn off the lights, the class is momentarily stunned, and, for some reason, the class quiets down. Darkening the room is my equivalent of throwing cold water on someone—but not as messy!

No Comparisons

Do any of you recall the time your parent compared you to your brother or sister? Or asked why you couldn't be like little June, the girl next door who seemed to do everything right? We all heard that and hated it, so let's not do it to our students. I remember telling one class how much more work I was able to accomplish with another class, and one girl put me in my place. She came up to me after class and said, "We are not the other class, and it hurts my feelings when you compare us. You remind me of my mother." Ouch! I felt terrible and vowed never to do that again.

I had one teacher friend who, although well-meaning, told each class it was her favorite. When students compared notes (and they will!), they discovered what she had done, which totally devalued her compliment.

Each class is an individual group with its own dynamics. Teaching would be boring if all classes were the same.

Never Attack Personally

A student's character should never be criticized, but rather the act you disapprove of. No teacher should ever tell children they are hopeless or bad or lazy. Rather than attacking their character, explain what they are doing that upsets you.

For example, if you catch a girl cheating on a test and she denies it, don't call her a liar and a cheat—rather, tell her that you are disappointed because she copied word-for-word from the book and didn't tell you the truth.

Distractions

When you sense there is student restlessness due to a pending fight, anxiety about a party after school, or even boredom, you need to distract them. I am not telling you to run around with a lamp shade on your head, but I am suggesting that you have an alternative to whatever you are doing. I always had a word search or some kind of math puzzle on hand. If there is a fight brewing, engage the potential "sparrers" with some kind of dialogue. You can also try turning off the lights to get their attention.

13

Knowing Your Audience

Group Dynamics

Be very cautious about the dynamics of your group. You can give the same lesson to a different class with totally different results. The chemistry of the group can only be determined after a couple of weeks. I did successful cooperative learning in groups of five with one class, but the same lesson bombed in another because I didn't realize that members of the second group were at war with one another. Often you can tell a joke to a more sophisticated group and you may get the expected chuckles. Other groups will hoot and get so carried away, you may actually think you have the potential to be a stand-up comic, when in reality they just wanted to be loud and obnoxious. (Yes, they can be obnoxious!)

Don't Play "I Gotcha"

Ah, little Liana is talking and not paying attention. Now is your chance to call on her and ask for the answer to the question you know she didn't hear, and show everyone in the room that talking does not pay. Good lesson for her? *No!* It is only going to humiliate her, and that is spiteful on your part. You are also setting a bad example and damaging the safe environment that you tried so hard to create. If she is really being disruptive, you may have to ask her to please pay attention and, granted, that may be a little embarrassing, but it won't be humiliating. Being told to be quiet is never as painful as being perceived as dumb.

Deceiving Looks

As a teacher of prejudice awareness, I am well aware that we all form judgments about people merely by how they look. It may be certain clothing, a certain swagger, or certain mannerisms. I have had these huge guys and tough-looking girls enter my classroom in the most challenging manner. Was I intimidated? Absolutely! But please profit from my years of experience. Looks mean absolutely nothing. The toughest-looking child very often is the sweetest but covers it by walking like a thug, and the reverse is true also. You assume that the darling little guy with the horn-rims who sits right near your desk is going to be your pet, but often he chose that seat because it is easier to torment you from there. So do not form any permanent opinions based on how a child looks. Very often, the students are just trying to make a statement to their peers, which may be totally misread by you.

Kids Have Bad Days, Too

Read body language. Sometimes a student will come into the room and slouch in her seat. Her eyes may be downcast, and you just sense she is having a bad day. Chances are you are right. I usually will whisper to the student, and ask her if she is OK. It's my way of saying, "I won't bother you." Many of my students lived in welfare hotels in New York, where I discovered that half the time, they didn't get to sleep because of the conditions in which they were trying to survive. Hopefully, teachers will share that kind of information with one another, so these children can feel safe within the classroom. I have often let students sleep, or even just tune out, but I would make them responsible for the work they missed. I've often had to stay after school with them to help them catch up.

Negative Attention Seekers

Many years ago, my purse was missing. I was trying to remain calm as I skimmed the classroom aisle by aisle in search of a clue before I went into total panic. And there, to my shock and dismay, hanging out of Todd's desk, was the strap of my purse. He stole my purse and wasn't even smart enough to cover his crime—or was he? He was a very bright little boy, but because of this act he had to stay after school, his parents were called in, and he was the center of attention. I noticed he was almost enjoying it.

I have since had similar experiences, though not as extreme. After many years of teaching, it becomes obvious that some students will do anything for attention, even if it means getting into trouble. If you sense you have such a student, I suggest you get the child to the counselor, but when possible, find positive ways to satisfy the need for attention that he or she so craves.

Hold Students to Different Standards

A principal of mine, Bea Ramirez, told me it was OK to hold different students to different standards.

A seriously disruptive child who had been kicked out of just about every class was contentedly sitting in the principal's office stuffing envelopes for a large mailing. I saw this as undermining the teachers by rewarding this student with a fun job. Ms. Ramirez pointed out that the child was sitting there quietly doing "work," and that if a child had broken a leg and could not partake in sports, she would likewise be sitting there stuffing envelopes.

This disruptive child suffered from an impairment. She could not control herself in class if her life depended on it. Ms. Ramirez let the student work with her, and then sent her back to class in a more relaxed mood.

The lesson? We seem to show much more compassion for students who have physical disabilities than those with emotional ones. Think about it.

If You Don't Try, You Can't Fail

If a child is failing in your class, don't just accept it—explore the possible causes. Perhaps the work is too difficult, perhaps the child has poor work habits and opts not to do any work, or perhaps computer games and TV have taken priority over books.

I have discovered another common pattern for you to store in your mind somewhere. Have you ever been afraid to take a test and as a result, you didn't study and failed? I have had students who became petrified before an exam and froze. A student doesn't study so that when she fails, she can rationalize that it was because she didn't open her books—not because she is dumb! You can't lose a race if you don't run, and you can't feel like a failure if you don't study. So the failure is face saving because it has a logical rationale.

Find out from parents if their children are studying at home. Parents should be aware of this problem and can help them study until their confidence is restored.

"Can We Really Be Anything We Want?"

Too often, a teacher will make a blanket statement to a group of students, telling them that they can be anything they dream of if they really try. What about those students who try and try but, sadly, do not have the ability to reach their goals? The severely learning-disabled girl who wants to be a doctor, or the mediocre athlete who wants to be a shortstop for the Mets, might need a reality check. As a teacher, I think it is irresponsible to give students false expectations when one knows they are not realistic. I don't believe in brutal honesty either, so I try to channel their interests into more realistic goals.

It is important to stress here that we must always encourage them to hold on to their dream. I just want them to know the importance of having a "Plan B" in case "Plan A" cannot be attained. Conversely, don't let the underachievers who score off the charts in every standardized test beat themselves up into believing they are failures. They too need a reality check to unleash whatever is holding them back.

Audio or Visual?

A friend of mine read me the description of the course she was taking at the local college. After reading it to me, she asked what I thought of it. I had to take the paper and read it to myself before I could give her my opinion. You see, I am a visual learner and so are many of your students. There are others who have difficulty reading concepts, yet grasp them immediately when they are orally explained. It is helpful for you to recognize these tendencies in your students.

A good idea is to have the class read some passages silently first and then ask for volunteers to read aloud. Often when students read aloud before reading silently, they have no idea what they have just read.

Respect Privacy

Very often, you want to know something that a student will not share with you. I have heard teachers cajoling students into telling them things about which they had no business asking, and most times with the best of intentions. Many times, you feel there is something your student is withholding from you, and you may be right. However, if your student is telling you there is nothing wrong, or doesn't want to talk about it, you have to leave it at that. Privacy must be respected. After assuring the student that you will always be there if she needs you, you must back off.

A Secret Is a Secret, Unless . . .

Sometime during your career a student may confide in you and ask you to promise you will not tell anyone what he or she has told you. Never make that promise—you may not be able to keep it. Remember, you are neither therapist nor doctor and can be held responsible for withholding information that can prove detrimental to a student's physical or mental health. I have had students share their feelings of suicide, physical and sexual abuse, drug use (either personal or familial), and unwanted pregnancies. Many secrets can remain between the two of you, but none of those just mentioned should. You will have to be honest with your student and explain that you must tell the authorities. I have had students feel betrayed by me, and let me tell you, it is an awful feeling. At the time, they experience only the betrayal and not the rescue.

Not too many years ago, a student who was a victim of abuse would not speak to me because I reported her case. I saw her 2 years later and was surprised when she gave me a bear hug that knocked the wind out of me. She had blossomed into a self-assured young woman, and guess what? She credited me for that. Of course, it is the foster mother with whom she eventually lived who deserved all the credit, but I took some of it anyway.

Ignore Reputation

Inevitably, teachers will offer you their condolences when they hear you have certain students in your class. These students' reputations precede them, and as you wait for them to enter the room to wreak havoc, you find yourself discovering the power of prayer. Many times they live up to your expectations, but most times, if you can erase what you heard from your mind, they are a piece of cake with you.

As teachers, we do not treat all our students the same. We enjoy some more than others, and perhaps—though we shouldn't—we get annoyed with others too quickly. Well, that goes the other way, too. Your students do not treat all their teachers the same, and you may be the one teacher they like and respect. Don't set yourself up for a self-fulfilling prophecy.

Permissive Versus Overly Permissive

Permissiveness is an attitude of accepting the childishness of children. Knowing that a young child can only sit for a certain period of time shows you respect the age of your student. Six-year-old children may roll on the floor laughing at the mere mention of the word "poop." So what? They are only six. Teenagers will laugh at anything dealing with their puberty. So what? They're teenagers.

Being overly permissive is another matter. Overpermissive behavior allows undesirable acts that bring about increasing demands and encourage negative behavior. If you allow students to stroll into your room at their leisure, don't be surprised if as the term progresses, they walk in as the dismissal bell rings. Not setting limits brings about these negative behaviors. It is up to you to know the difference between being permissive and overly permissive, and to point it out to your students.

Cultural Differences

When I began teaching, a little boy was acting rude and I was giving him a stern lecture. He wouldn't look me in the eye and it infuriated me. I don't remember which Central American country he was from, but he had been taught there that it was disrespectful to look a teacher in the eye—respect was shown by looking down. In a similar vein, one of my Asian students told me it was considered improper to challenge the teacher.

Acknowledging, accepting, and appreciating cultural differences can prevent serious misunderstandings. You might suggest to your principal that it would be a good topic for a faculty conference, especially if you are in a multicultural school. If you have a culturally diverse class, seize the opportunity to have your students share cultural differences unique to their particular group.

A friend of mine suggests that teachers who have multilingual classes learn some common phrases in the native tongues of their students. It puts the students at ease and allows them to chuckle when you mispronounce a word or phrase in their language. (Don't be offended if they laugh at you; it is really making them feel confident because they know something you don't.)

Quality, Not Quantity

You have a student who hands in a neatly written 12-page paper, although you asked for a 1-page essay. Don't you feel awful when after you read it, you don't like it? Many children feel they will get more approval if they hand in *a lot.* You have to stress that quality is more important than quantity. I always chuckle when I assign a 150-word paper and I see the little numbers in the margin where the student counted the number of words. I smile because I remember doing it, believing that my teacher would count every word. I guess kids don't change—they still think we don't have a life!

Confusing Neatness With Responsibility

When a student hands in a neatly printed assignment, we often think a lot of effort went into it. In many cases it did, but that should not be an assumption. Conversely, penmanship that looks like that of a chimp should not be devalued. Difficult-to-read penmanship is often something a student can't correct. I do encourage those with poor penmanship to use a word processor if they have access to one, so my life will be easier.

Describe a Fight to a Potential Pugilist

In my school, physical violence was much too commonplace. There was a hardly a day that went by when there wasn't a fight. I used to think that these children just wanted to fight to show how tough they were. But after a few years I realized that in most cases it was not the two fighters who wanted to engage in battle, but rather the other children who wanted to stand on the sidelines where it was safe. I have seen children push two other students into one another hoping to get a good fight going. I have heard instigating that would prompt *me* to put up *my* dukes. Kids will use any strategy to goad the fighters to punch it out.

What I do is gather the two potential fighters and point out how everyone wants to see their blood, and how their "friends" will not let up until one of them is hurt. (I am usually quite graphic here.) In 9 out of 10 cases, it is apparent that neither one wants to fight, so I give them an out by blaming the spectators. They walk away relieved that they were given an out.

The Sound-Off Minute

This strategy works only once, because it is a quick-fix solution that is not meant to remedy deep, recurring problems. But take it for what it's worth and use it with discretion.

When I have a student alone in my room who is really upset with me, I offer every student's dream—that is, the opportunity to say anything to me that she wants, with a promise that I will not in any way punish her afterwards. The only drawback is that she has exactly 60 seconds to sound off and get it off her chest. The initial reaction is, "Huh? I can say anything?" I explain that it is an uninterrupted minute, free of reprisal. What usually happens is a student will gripe and whine and tell you that you are the worst teacher on the entire planet and so on. When you say, "OK, the minute is up," there is usually a giggle and most of the anger is dissipated.

Overgrading

You have a wonderful student who shines, so you give her a grade of 100% on her report card. But 100% means perfect, and so there is no room for improvement. The danger of giving students such a high grade is that the only way they can go on their next report card is down. I usually explain that to them, as well as to their parents. I know teachers who give 98s and 99s the first term, and it creates tremendous stress for the student to maintain that level. There is nothing wrong with a 95, and it does offer the opportunity for improvement.

Confidence Grading

On the other side of the coin is the student who really should fail but tries so hard. I will often pass the child with a barely passing grade so as not to discourage him from keeping up a necessary level of determination and effort.

I do get disturbed when a teacher gives the same student a 90% because he tried hard. That is unfair. A 90 is well above average, and effort should not take precedence over quality. My 65 tells other teachers as well as my student that the work is marginal but passing. Anything else is really being dishonest to everyone and will only ensure the student gets a hard dose of reality down the road.

It's That Time of the Month

Women and men reading this will probably have different reactions.

When a girl asks her teacher if she can get a sanitary napkin, how can anyone say no? It's easy—once you discover she has her period 29 out of 30 days of the month with different teachers.

Also, men sometimes fall prey to the "I can't do any work, it's that time of the month" complaint, as a young girl's face contorts in agony. Guys: Don't be a pushover—be a little suspicious. Because men don't menstruate, they believe the worst. In some cases, young women *do have* bad cramps, and if this pattern is apparent, you should refer her to the school nurse because she may have a serious problem. (Male teachers might ask a female colleague to assess the situation.)

But we must not treat menstruation as a disability. If we do, women will not have a fair shot in the real world if they are "disabled" once a month. Because I am a woman, I am able to talk more freely with my girls. I have had girls ask to go home because they have their periods, and I would whisper that I also have mine, that I will stick out the day, and that I know they can, too. Menstruation is a natural part of life and should be treated as such. There are many painkillers that can alleviate the cramps, but again I must stress that if a student is in obvious pain, you must make sure her parents are informed, and you should bring her to the school nurse for evaluation.

USING YOUR
SUPPORT SYSTEM

Teaching is an "interdependent" profession. Without the help of parents, fellow teachers, administrators, and support staff, your job would be overwhelmingly complex. You need to develop strong relationships with these people to make a school work. Our profession, though very rewarding, can also be difficult and frustrating. What is important is teamwork, and for your team to be successful, you must be a team player. Remember: Although there may be disagreements, you are all on the same side with the same goals. You all want your students to succeed.

14

Working With Parents

Meet Parents Right Away

Parents are a wonderful asset and certainly should be utilized. Very often parents never even meet the teacher until Open School Day or after being summoned. I think it is very important for you to put faces to the parents of your students. They also get to meet you and see how terrific you are. As a parent, I always wanted to meet my daughter's teachers, but I rarely did because of my busy schedule. One year, her teacher invited all the parents to come to school one evening. She told us her objectives, gave us a short demonstration lesson, and asked us if there was anything she should know about our child. Because she scheduled a specific day and time, we were all there. It is like your friend who says, "Drop over any time." You rarely do, unless he or she sets a specific time. So you might try that with your student's parents.

I suggest you think twice about telling them to drop in at any time. Of course, *you* wouldn't mind, but your student might shrivel up into a red-faced ball.

Send Home an Introduction

Many parents cannot spare the time to come to school except when required, so a nice touch is to send home a letter of introduction. Tell them about yourself and what you hope to accomplish this year with their child. Encourage them not to hesitate to call you at school if they have any concerns. Here I would suggest you give them the school number rather than your home number, because some parents call for every little thing. You might close your letter by asking if they have any insights into their child that would make his or her educational experience more productive. Now, what parent wouldn't enjoy getting a letter like that? And starting off on such a good foot surely can't hurt.

Getting Parents Involved

Every school has active parents whom everyone else counts on to do all the work. However, it is important to encourage *all* parents to be involved in their child's schooling. Some parents are actually intimidated by that expectation and back away. Calling parents once in a while can make them feel comfortable with you. You might ask if they would join the class on a trip, or share some time helping with reading groups, or perhaps talk to the class about the work they do. However, before you invite one to lecture, ask your student how he or she feels about it. Some kids are embarrassed by their parent's presence, whereas others are thrilled. When the parents do help, a short thank-you note is always appropriate and thoughtful.

Call Both Parents

How many times do teachers say, "OK, that's it! I am going to call your *mother!*" I always believed that parenting involved two parents. Yes, sometimes there is only one parent, but often there are two. As a mother, I feel it is an unfair burden if a teacher assumes I am the only parent responsible for our child. I don't want my child, or anyone else's, to get the impression that the responsibility all falls on *Mother*.

We should tell our students we are going to call home, or call a parent. Always "calling the mother" is unfair to mothers and relieves fathers of the joint responsibility. Worse yet, it causes our students to internalize erroneous gender roles.

It is a good idea for you to find out with whom your student lives. It could be a grandparent, foster parent, or even an institution.

Students at Parent Conferences?

Whether students should be present at parent conferences is a debatable question to which I can answer both yes and no and be correct. This is really a judgment call. Many teachers demand that their students come with their parents, while others forbid it. I do neither. I tell my students that my practice is to speak to Mom and Dad alone, but they may feel free to join in after our conversation. I tell them that in advance so they do not think I am saying horrible things about them. In fact, when they join us I will say something glowing so they all leave on an "up."

The reason I want to confer with parents in private is because sometimes the *parents* may not be able to talk openly in front of the child. Parents may be contemplating a divorce, there may be a death in the family, or they may feel out of control regarding their child—any number of things that could make the child's presence inhibiting. When they're all talked out, ask the parents if you may discuss what they have shared with you with their child now, or perhaps at a later date.

I had a student, Brenda, who was nearly perfect, and I didn't think I had to talk to the mother privately, but because I had told the class I do that with everyone, I had to. Well, in that conference I learned that Brenda was anorexic. Brenda wanted it to remain a secret, but her mother thought it was too important not to share with me. And the mother admitted that she would not have told me this in her daughter's presence.

As I said, many teachers feel it is necessary for the child to be sitting there so everything will be out in the open—but will it really be?

Assuring Parents

Parents love their kids. They may not always like their behavior and may even say terrible things about them, but don't you dare think of agreeing with them! Often parents, like their children, need to know you are on their side.

I have had terribly hostile parents come up to me and I would react in kind. Nothing was accomplished because we were both defending ourselves. Once you let them know you are not attacking their parenting skills, one layer of the armor goes down. I had a mother come to me with a real attitude. Just as we were about to square off, I put my hand on hers, and said, "Ms. Johnson, we both care about Jack. I know you teach him right from wrong, and please know he is very special to me, too." Suddenly, it was as if I were talking to a new parent. I found out many painful things I needed to know about Jack that explained his erratic behavior. She shared information she never would have, had she perceived me as an adversary.

Another strategy is to say things to the student in front of the parent such as:

> "You probably think your parents and I think we know it all and are always telling you what to do."
> "Do you know how hard it is to be a parent?"
> "Do you know that your parents go to bed at night and worry about you?"

Parents love it (and you), and some children do gain insight.

The Defensive Parent

Do any of you remember when you were a child and the teacher made a phone call home and you knew you were in trouble? Well, bad news: Now you are the teacher and you may still get in trouble for a phone call home. You may call enabling parents who will immediately put you on the defensive and not believe a word you say. You may hear something like, "Little Samantha said you are picking on her for nothing and so is every other teacher, and I want to know what you are going to do about it." I always expected, naïvely, that a parent would support me when I had difficulty with a child. However, when I became a parent, I too knew I had given birth to the perfect angel. If there was a complaint about her from a teacher, my gut reaction was a desire to inflict physical harm on him for practicing blasphemy. Fortunately, I learned to listen to and support the teacher and work toward solutions that would better the situation.

Please be prepared for the parents who enable their children by always defending them, right or wrong. The reality is that most parents are wonderfully cooperative and helpful, but I want you to be prepared for the occasional difficult one.

Parents and Homework

Very often, well-meaning parents do their child's homework. They seem to have a hard time drawing the line between helping and doing. If you notice the caliber of a student's work seems to be above her ability, you might speak to the parent. I encourage parents not to do work *for* their child but, rather, *with* their child. It is important for a parent to check homework, help the child prepare for exams, and help explain something the child doesn't understand. But doing the homework for one's child, when she doesn't understand it, is a disservice to that child.

I might also mention here again that your assignments make a statement about you. They tell whether you are smart, boring, creative, unrealistic, or lazy.

Children as Dream Fulfillers

As parents, we all have dreams for our children. Often they are the dreams we couldn't fulfill for ourselves, or they are dreams that we truly believe will make our child happy. Sometimes, we teachers have to rescue our students from their own parents' expectations. All children have limitations, and too often a parent refuses to see them and pushes a child too far. I have seen students suffering from depression because they feel they are disappointing their parents. No child should be made to feel that way, and you have to make that perfectly clear to a parent who you feel is creating this problem. I suggest you have the guidance counselor handle it.

Stuyvesant High School in New York City is one of the most prestigious high schools in the country. Needless to say, there is fierce competition among applicants to the school. It specializes in math and science, and, too often, I see students who have average aptitudes in these subjects cram, take expensive courses, and stress out because their parents will be upset if they don't get in. I have also had other students who are very bright but hated math and science, yet chose to go to that school because it fulfilled their parents' dreams rather than their own.

Parents Knowing More Than You

Most parents finished high school and therefore believe their experiences make them experts in the field of teaching. They will tell you what you are doing wrong and sometimes even forget to praise you when you are doing something right.

Don't get defensive, unless of course they become utterly offensive, in which case it might be a good idea to have a discussion in the presence of your principal. Just smile and thank them for their advice. Ever notice that when Johnny can't read, it's because of the terrible teacher, but when he is a scholar it is because he inherited his parents' great genes?

Beware of the Answering Machine

Believe it or not, I actually began teaching before the advent of the answering machine. (And I am still alive.) When we need to call home, we now hear singing messages, humorous messages, and unending messages before we can leave our own message for what we hope will be a parent. It is tempting fate to leave a message in which you tell parents that their child is in deep trouble. Would you blame your student for "accidentally" pushing the erase button?

I suggest you leave a message merely stating that you would like to speak to a parent. Use as upbeat a voice as you can muster. Then say that you will assume they did not get the message if they do not call back and that you will try again later. After all, how many accidents can a student have before someone gets suspicious?

15

Working With the School Support Team

Cooperative Teacher Input

Several of my colleagues and I used to arrive at school an hour early to share concerns and strategies regarding our students. It is helpful when a teacher informs you that a student has some personal problems or can share some information about his or her interaction with classmates. It's always helpful to know where your students need enrichment. However, you must remember not to share specific information that would be violating a confidence. An example would be the girl in my class who was upset because she was pregnant and didn't want anyone to know. I felt it inappropriate to share that information. However, I told my colleagues that she had some pressing personal problems.

Buddy Teacher

Sometimes every trick we have tried doesn't work, and we feel ourselves about to go on "automatic" and fear we will say and do things we will regret—like murder! A good idea is to prearrange with another teacher to be a "buddy." This teacher will take a student out of your room for you, or you can merely tell your student to go to your colleague's room. You might find a student particularly resistant, in which case you'd give him a choice. "Either you go to Mr.

Tenney's room, or you go to the dean or principal!" They usually opt for choice number one and they are surprisingly well behaved there. Don't take it personally. It is not unlike the young child who will eat liver at a friend's house but will fast indefinitely at yours.

Confronting Other Teachers

This one is a toughie! Students will often confide in me about difficulties they are having with another teacher. Usually I will try to mediate the situation and arm my student with strategies, many of which I've presented already. It is important for your students to know that sometimes life is not fair, and that extends into the classroom. Be very careful not to speak badly about another teacher because that is highly unprofessional. I have heard students gripe about certain teachers, and I know their gripes are legitimate. I explain that in the real world we are always going to have to deal with difficult people, and school is an early training ground. Our students cannot just explode if they don't like it when one teacher takes off 3 points for a missed homework although another teacher doesn't.

As an advocate for students, we are remiss if we do not defend the child who is legitimately being unfairly treated after trying all reasonable actions. You must then intercede and try to mediate the situation with your colleague. If you cannot do that, and I know it is difficult, speak to an administrator. You may not win a popularity contest with that teacher, but you will have done what we are all paid to do and that is to be an advocate for students.

Teacher Competition

In all professions, there is competition among coworkers, and teaching is no exception. You need to know your audience when you work with students *and* colleagues. Most teachers I have met are generous of spirit and willing to share and grow professionally with their colleagues. There will be some who "know it all," some who will not share their tips with you, and some who may even criticize your lessons unfairly. If you feel a colleague fits the latter description, unless he or she affects your ability to teach, don't let it bother you. It takes too much energy to wonder why Mr. Smith or Ms. Bell neglected to tell you that your class is waiting for you in a different room.

Helping Substitute Teachers

What do a combat soldier and a substitute teacher have in common? If you said they both should earn hazardous duty pay, you are right!

When I went on child-care leave, I did some subbing and thought it would be fun. Often it was, but once in a while, I had to fight the urge to run out of the school ranting and raving. The students actually had the nerve to treat me just as I had treated subs when I was their age! To many students, having a substitute teacher is like having a baby-sitter, and we all know that means getting away with murder, or at least less schoolwork. So my suggestion here is to show compassion for soon-to-be-tormented subs by preparing for them. It really works to your advantage. Upon your return, you want your students to fall right back into the routines you've established.

Have a seating chart available for subs so they can see who is present right away. Have them call the attendance as well as pass around a sheet for your students to sign. I have had students yell "Present!" for every absentee and anyone cutting class. By having their signatures on a sheet of paper, you can verify who was actually in the room. Also, have your hall pass in a conspicuous place and ask the subs to make sure they inform you who left the room during class.

The most important thing to prepare is your lesson plan. After all, most of us don't know the day before that we will be ill, and you don't want to be caught without leaving a good lesson. There is no rule saying you must leave a lesson that follows what you did the day before—just have a good lesson waiting for your sub. Because I taught sex education and prejudice awareness, a substitute could not teach my lessons unless he or she was trained therein, and the likelihood of that was almost nil. But even when I taught English and K–8, I always had a backup "generic" lesson plan. I suggest you have one, too.

It should be a lesson that your students will understand and can work with somewhat independently. I used to use self-actualization lessons. For example, I would have the students write about different kinds of conflict and relate one to their own experience. I would have handouts for them to read about different conflicts and have them figure out ways to resolve them. Substitutes can use as much or as little as they see fit.

I had one sub who, after the first part, engaged the class in a wonderful discussion and thanked me for my good lesson. I, in good conscience, could not accept the credit because he established the rapport that allowed that to happen.

Any work you have your class do in your absence should be graded by you! This way your students know you take the sub's work just as seriously as your own.

Preparing Your Students for Your Absence

If you know you are going to be absent, let your students know in no uncertain terms that you left work for them and you expect it to be done just as they would do it with you. I would also appeal to their human side and tell them that you expect them to treat a substitute teacher with utmost respect. My students were told that I had instructed any sub to give me the names of anyone who misbehaved and that there would be consequences to pay. I finally would plead with them to be nice and not embarrass me.

Evaluating Substitute Teachers

I suggest you inform your school of great substitutes and request them in your absence. Conversely, if you have a bad experience with a sub, you might ask your principal not to let him or her cover for you again. I still shudder at the sub who allowed my class to go wild because he couldn't control them and refused help—even when it was offered to him. Often in difficult schools, having a warm body is the only requirement needed to be hired as a substitute, and I find that a disservice to everyone involved, especially the students.

Getting Along With the "Boss"

The principal is where the buck stops. It is very important for you to have a good relationship with him or her. Some principals are easier to get along with than others, but my advice to you is make every effort to get into his or her good graces. Just as we do not like all our students with equal relish, neither do principals like all their staff members.

For this strategy, I must admit I cheated. I went right to my friend Pearl, who is a principal, and asked her what would cause a principal to dislike a teacher's performance. She cited the following: lateness, irregular attendance, unpreparedness, idle or unruly classes, sloppy record keeping, noticeably poor student achievement, an unwarranted number of student-behavior problems, legitimate parent complaints—to name just a few.

A word of caution in your apple-polishing campaign: You want your principal to like you, but don't promise to spin straw into gold. If your principal asks you to do something you really cannot do (such as leading a chorus although you are tone-deaf), don't accept the assignment in the hope that your willingness will be appreciated so much that your poor performance will be overlooked. If the principal insists, at least you gave fair warning! On the other hand, if you want to be noticed and praised (yes, we all enjoy that!), do volunteer for tasks that you know you can do and that will serve the school while showing off your talents.

The Really Important People

Anyone teaching for more than an hour knows the best friends you can have are the school secretary and the custodians. No matter what they do to you, smile and say "Thank you." The secretary often runs the school. She knows where everything is and what paperwork has to be done for you to get raises, benefits, and the like. She also does the payroll. Need I say more? Seriously, the secretary is someone whose help you always need. Let her know how much you appreciate her.

There will always come a time or a crisis when you will need the custodian. Perhaps you are locked out of your room, a window got shattered, your shelves collapsed, or little Louise just upchucked her lunch. If you have a good relationship with the custodian, he might run instead of walk.

Security guards, aides, nurses, guidance counselors, and all support staff are part of that team that makes your school work, and everyone should be appreciated and utilized. You should know the proper procedures and chain of command to reach these people when needed.

In the event of suspected abuse, know the procedure to report whatever you think is relevant. Being remiss may bring harm to a student as well as a lawsuit to your school.

PARTING SHOTS

In June, when the year is winding down and everyone is anxious for the final bell and 2 chalk-free months, hopefully you will be able to look back and feel rewarded by your experiences. You may have touched some young people, and you may even be the person they remember in their later years when they reminisce about that wonderful teacher who made a difference. Following are a few final thoughts I'd like to share with you before I end. And once again, thank you for being that special person—a *teacher*.

16

See You Next Year!

Is Teaching What You Really Want to Do?

I am a firm believer that teaching is a talent. Some of us have it, and unfortunately some of us don't. We all have talents and we have to recognize where they lie. I yearn to be a rock singer, but I can't carry a tune. Conversely, many rock stars would bore a class to death. You may be brilliant, but if you are not communicating with your students, nor finding pleasure in what you are doing, perhaps you should reevaluate your career choice. If you are enjoying your job but are finding the first few years difficult, don't despair—you're getting your feet wet. However, if you are unable to control a class after 4 or 5 years, and dread going in—consider being a rock singer!

When All Else Fails, Buy Pizza

Sometimes we've tried every strategy in this book and then some. Your students are pouting and thinking you were put on Earth to torment them. Perhaps they are right, but they do not have to know that. Here's a sure way of making things better: Buy a few pizzas!

I don't know why, but a slice of pizza elevates you to "the coolest teacher in the world." Granted, on our salaries we cannot do it too often, but a party of any kind can suffice. I tell my class that I think we need some healing, and an olive branch would not be received as well as some good old-fashioned junk food!

Keep in Touch

Before school ends, take the addresses of your students, so you can keep in touch with them over the years. I still send them Season's Greetings cards and hear from many. Hearing about their personal growth over the years, and knowing you were part of it, is what teaching is all about.

Only a Few More Months Till Summer Vacation

I warn you right now that you are going to hear from others how easy your job is because you get summers off. To those people who would belittle my job because I have so much time off I would say, "If you are my friend, you're happy for me—if you're not, eat your heart out!"

I know and you know that teaching is exhausting, and the summer vacation is needed for you to merely reenergize. So have a wonderful summer, do fun things for yourself, and be proud of your accomplishments—*you earned it!*

Suggested Readings

Artman, J. (1989). *Insights.* Carthage, IL: Good Apple.

Canfield, J., & Wells, H. (1976). *100 ways to enhance self-concept in the classroom.* Englewood Cliffs, NJ: Prentice Hall.

Charles, C. M. (1981). *Building classroom discipline.* White Plains, NY: Longman.

Chase, J., & Chase, C. (1993). *Tips from the trenches.* Lancaster, PA: Technomic.

Christopher, C. J. (1992). *Nuts and bolts.* Lancaster, PA: Technomic.

Faber, A., & Mazlish, E. (1982). *How to talk so kids will listen.* New York: Avon.

Fisher, R., & Ury, W. (1983). *Getting to yes: Negotiating agreement without giving in.* New York: Penguin.

Ford, C. W. (1994). *We can all get along: 50 steps you can take to help end racism.* New York: Dell.

Ginott, H. (1975). *Teacher and child.* New York: Avon.

Golub, J. N. (1994). *Activities for an interactive classroom.* Urbana, IL: National Council of Teachers of English.

Kreidler, W. J. (1984). *Creative conflict resolution: More than 200 activities for keeping peace in the classroom.* Glenview, IL: Scott, Foresman.

Lickona, T. (1991). *Educating for character.* New York: Bantam.

Lighter, D. (1995). *Gentle discipline.* Deephaven, MN: Meadowbrook.

Pipher, M. (1994). *Reviving Ophelia.* New York: Ballantine.

Ray, P. (1990). *Resolving conflict creatively.* New York: Educators for Social Responsibility.

CORWIN
PRESS

The Corwin Press logo—a raven striding across an open book—
represents the happy union of courage and learning. We are a
professional-level publisher of books and journals for K-12 educators, and we are committed to creating and providing resources that
embody these qualities. Corwin's motto is "Success for All Learners."